WILLIAMS-SONOMA

starters
new healthy kitchen

RECIPES
Georgeanne Brennan

GENERAL EDITOR
Chuck Williams

PHOTOGRAPHY
Dan Goldberg & Ben Dearnley

FREE PRESS

NEW YORK · LONDON · TORONTO · SYDNEY

contents

About this book

The books of the New Healthy Kitchen series offer simple and appealing ways to enjoy a diet rich in fruits, vegetables, legumes, and grains.

In our modern world, we are blessed with an abundance of food, from superb raw ingredients to highly processed convenience foods. But it is all too easy to get stuck in a food rut or make an unhealthy choice. Because the kinds of foods you eat directly affect your overall health and energy level, adding a wide selection of fresh produce and whole grains to your diet is one of the best things you can do to eat more healthfully and live better.

The recipes in this book are organized in a new way: by the color of the vegetable or fruit used in the dish. In the pages that follow, you'll discover how each color group offers a different benefit to your overall health. But on a more basic level, thinking about color is an easy way to make sure you are eating all the fresh produce you need. If you remember to eat at least one fruit or vegetable from each color group every few days, as part of a meal, snack, or dessert, you will be well on your way to a fresh and varied diet. A chapter of recipes featuring whole grains and legumes rounds out this cookbook, offering enticing dishes in which to enjoy these supremely wholesome foods.

The New Healthy Kitchen series will help you bring color and creativity into your kitchen, making it easy to enjoy a wide range of fresh fruits, vegetables, and whole grains in your meals every day.

Eating the rainbow

Purple and blue fruits and vegetables contain fiber, vitamins, and phytochemicals that promote heart health; help memory function; lower the risk of some cancers; promote urinary tract health; and boost immunity

Green fruits and vegetables contain fiber, vitamins, and phytochemicals that lower the risk of breast, prostate, lung, and other cancers; promote eye health; help build strong bones and teeth; and boost immunity

White and tan fruits and vegetables contain fiber, vitamins, and phytochemicals that promote heart health; help maintain healthful cholesterol levels; lower the risk of breast, lung, and other cancers; and slow cholesterol absorption

Red fruits and vegetables contain fiber, vitamins, and phytochemicals that promote heart health; help memory function; lower the risk of certain cancers; promote urinary tract health; and boost immunity

Yellow and orange fruits and vegetables contain fiber, vitamins, and phytochemicals that promote heart health; promote eye health; lower the risk of some cancers; and boost immunity

Brown whole grains, legumes, seeds, and nuts include fiber, vitamins, and phytonutrients that lower blood cholesterol levels and reduce the risk of colon and other cancers, diabetes, heart disease, and stroke

Adapted from educational materials of the Produce for Better Health Foundation

The new healthy kitchen

The simple act of eating has become more complex today because of the abundance of food—especially prepared foods—available to us, plus a growing number of diet plans and theories. This cookbook takes the approach that healthful food is fresh, seasonal, and, most important, *good* food: the kind that delights the senses and makes eating one of life's greatest pleasures.

Other essential tenets of the New Healthy Kitchen philosophy include choosing high-quality fresh ingredients, cooking them in ways that bring out their flavors, and serving dishes and meals in simple, pleasing ways.

In recent years, we've been inundated with mixed messages about what's healthy and what's not. Eggs were condemned, then earned a reprieve. We were told to cut out all fat, then later we were told to go ahead and eat as much meat as we liked—as long as we avoided carbs like bread and pasta.

Set aside all the controversy and mixed messages, and you will find that a more reasonable way to eat is not to focus exclusively on carbohydrates, fat grams, or calories, or to gorge on "good" foods while avoiding "bad" foods, but rather to eat a variety of well-prepared foods in reasonable portions and to enjoy and savor them.

This book will help you do just that, by emphasizing foods that we often neglect in our diet: vegetables, fruits, legumes, and grains. Despite our best intentions, these are the foods that quickly fall by the wayside unless we make a focused effort to include them in our diets every day.

Our bodies crave the vitamins and minerals provided by a wide range of plant foods. But our modern diet is remarkably

restricted in the kind of plant foods we eat. With the abundance of all types of food freely at our disposal, we tend to overindulge in concentrated sources of energy, especially animal fats. We also gravitate toward carbohydrates, which are excellent sources of quick energy, but unfortunately some of our most common carbohydrates, such as refined white flour and white rice, are stripped of the wholesome nutrients found in whole grains.

While taking a daily multivitamin or eating a vitamin-fortified breakfast cereal is a good idea, popping a variety of supplement pills isn't the optimal solution to a lack of vitamins and minerals in the diet. Allowing your body to extract these nutrients from different foods is in fact the best way of

getting what you need, in the form in which your body is naturally designed to use it.

In addition to supplying us with essential vitamins, minerals, and fiber, fruits and vegetables are rich in phytochemicals, beneficial compounds found only in plants. In many cases, phytochemicals are what give fruits and vegetables their distinctive colors and flavors. In fact, the colors themselves are the best clues to tell us which phytonutrients the foods contain: a yellow-skinned apple offers different benefits from a red-skinned apple or a green-skinned one.

Ideally, a good portion of the food you eat daily should come from another group of plant foods: grains, legumes, seeds, and nuts. These foods are rich in fiber, protein, complex carbohydrates, and minerals.

A portion of the grains you eat should be unrefined, as close to their natural state as possible. This means whole-wheat (wholemeal) flour and brown rice instead of white.

The recipes in this book aim to help you bring a range of bright, health-enhancing, fresh plant foods into your diet, and so are organized by color: Purple and Blue, Green, White and Tan, Yellow and Orange, and Red, plus a Brown chapter, which includes grains and legumes. Each produce chapter begins with a chart showing which fruits and vegetables are at their peak of ripeness each season. The recipes are quick, simple, and straightforward, designed for modern cooks who haven't much spare time on their hands but want to bring a colorful bounty of fresh and healthful foods to their table every day.

Fruits & vegetables

Fruits and vegetables are the cornerstone of a healthy diet. They are also some of the most beautiful and delicious foods on the planet—a boon to both the eye and the palate, with tastes and textures that range from bitter greens to sweet cherries. The recipes in *Starters* will inspire you to add new fruits and vegetables to your meals and reap the benefits of their vitamins, minerals, and phytochemicals.

In the early years of the twentieth century, one after another, the various vitamins and minerals we now know are essential to maintaining good health and fighting disease were discovered. We are now entering into a similarly exciting era of discovery, as we learn about the roles that phytochemicals play in our bodies.

These protective compounds, which are believed to number in the thousands, work alone and in combination with one another and with nutrients. They work in different ways. For example, some phytochemicals act as antioxidants, protecting the body by neutralizing unstable oxygen molecules (known as free radicals) that damage cells and promote disease. Regularly eating plant foods rich in antioxidants can reduce the incidence of various cancers, heart disease, impaired vision, and other health problems.

Fruits and vegetables from each of the color groups provide us with a different combination of phytonutrients, each playing a unique role in fighting disease and promoting health and well-being.

By eating fruit and vegetables at their peak of ripeness, you will not only be pleasing your palate, but you will also be giving your body the benefit of all the healthy nutrients that these foods contain.

Grains & legumes

Grains and legumes have long played a key role in the human diet. In Asia, no meal is complete without rice, while beans are seldom absent from the Mexican table. American diners have long been accustomed to eating rice or a white bread roll as part of dinner. Lately, however, there has been a rising interest in healthier whole grains, from basic brown rice to homey barley and exotic quinoa.

Perhaps the interest comes in reaction to the recent low-carb diet fad, which made white breads and pastas taboo. Whatever the cause, making a shift from refined white grains to unrefined brown ones is a welcome development from a health standpoint.

Grains—as well as legumes, nuts, and seeds—are good sources of fiber, which keeps our digestive system in working order and helps regulate the cholesterol levels in our blood. But in our modern diet, grains are usually refined, with the fiber-rich hull and the nutrient-rich germ removed.

In the New Healthy Kitchen, recipes focusing on grains and legumes are grouped in a chapter called Brown. These foods come in a variety of colors, but you can think of them as "brown" to remind yourself that they should be as close to their natural state as possible—not stripped of nutrients, texture, and color.

The recipes in this book encourage you to try a variety of grains, such as barley and bulgur, in their whole forms. It's worthwhile experimenting with other, less common types of whole grains, too, such as quinoa (pronounced KEEN-wah), an ancient grain from South America, or millet.

Legumes, which are the seeds of plants that split open when dried, include peas, beans, lentils, and peanuts. They contain fiber, complex carbohydrates, phosphorus, and iron, plus plenty of protein: ¼ cup cooked dried beans or 1 tablespoon peanut butter equals 1 ounce of cooked meat, fish, or poultry. And they are available in a wide range of appealing colors and shapes, from yellow chickpeas (garbanzo beans) and green split peas to red, green, yellow, brown, and tiny black lentils.

Seeds belonging to this same category include flaxseed, sesame seeds, and all varieties of tree nuts, from almonds to walnuts to cashews. These are rich in omega-3 fatty acids and high in fiber, which has been shown to help keep cholesterol levels down. Nuts are a good source of the antioxidant vitamin E, which is beneficial to heart health.

Other ingredients

The colorful eating philosophy of the New Healthy Kitchen revolves mainly around fruits and vegetables, with an emphasis on whole grains and legumes as well. But it doesn't exclude a variety of meats and dairy products. Along with herbs and spices and healthy oils, these ingredients help round out recipes and can be used to add flavor, interest, texture, and nutrients to healthy dishes.

Meat, dairy, and other animal foods appeal to our bodies' craving for nutrient-rich calories, but it's easy to overindulge in these ingredients, especially when you lead a typically sedentary modern lifestyle. The secret is to find a healthy balance in using and enjoying these ingredients.

Certain meats can play the role of seasoning. Only a little bacon, pancetta, or prosciutto can lend flavor and interest to otherwise meatless dishes. Used as an accent in a first course of soup, salad, or pasta, or as the focus of a festive canapé, meats and cheeses play an important role in this cookbook, bringing satisfying flavors and texture to dishes that also feature a colorful vegetable or grain.

When choosing meat and cheese to prepare your meals, look for unprocessed cheeses, organic poultry and eggs, and naturally raised beef, pork, and lamb. When chosen and prepared with care at home, these forms of meat and dairy are far more wholesome than prepared, processed foods loaded with preservatives and additives.

While too much fat adds excessive calories to the diet, a certain amount of fat is essential for the body to function properly. Fat also adds a satisfying texture to foods and gives us the sensation of being satiated, which helps us to avoid overeating. Most of the recipes in this book use olive oil and canola oil as the primary fats for cooking. Along with grape seed, these oils have been proven beneficial, thanks to their monounsaturated fat content, which raises the level of good cholesterol and lowers the bad. Nut oils are rich in healthful omega-3 fats and add excellent flavor to salads and vegetable dishes, as do extra-virgin olive oils.

Dairy foods that are high in saturated fat, such as butter and cheese, should be used judiciously. Many dairy ingredients that are used in this cookbook in dressings or as a garnish, such as sour cream or mayonnaise, also come in light and low-fat versions. Yogurt is a naturally healthy part of any diet. It contributes not only calcium and protein to a dish, but also enzymes that help us with digestion. In some cases it can replace a richer dairy ingredient as a garnish.

Just a small amount of Parmesan or aged pecorino cheese brings out the flavor of a pasta or an appetizer without tipping the scales too far toward richness. And many fresh cheeses, such as feta and ricotta, are naturally low in fat, and yet make a delicious contribution to many dishes.

Herbs and spices are essential flavor boosters in the healthy kitchen. A simple scattering of minced fresh basil, parsley, or chives, for example, adds both color and an intense flavor note to so many different foods, and green antioxidants as well.

Some herbs, such basil and parsley, lose flavor and, of course, texture when dried, and are best used in their fresh state. But herbs with tougher leaves, such as thyme and rosemary, maintain their bright taste in dried form. As a general rule, add dried herbs to foods during the cooking process, and fresh herbs at the end of cooking. Rub fresh or dried herbs between your fingers to bring out their full flavor.

For best flavor, buy spices in their whole state and grind them yourself in a spice grinder or an electric coffee grinder used just for that purpose. Dried spices and seeds, such as cumin and fennel, will improve in flavor if toasted lightly in a small dry skillet before they are ground. This awakens the spice's distinctive flavor and fragrance.

Vinegar, citrus juice, and citrus zest are other important flavorings in the healthy kitchen. These ingredients contribute an acidic note to a dish, which boosts other flavors without making a dish heavy.

Creating the healthy meal

A healthy meal can begin with a soup, a salad, or an interesting platter of hors d'oeuvres. The fresh, simple recipes featured in *Starters*—many of which can be doubled to serve as light main dishes—will guide you toward making every meal not only healthful but also original and delightful. Eating a variety of fresh foods and incorporating all the colors of the rainbow are the two keys to a vibrant table.

Choosing produce at its peak of freshness, flavor, and nutrient levels is the first step in creating a healthy meal. This can mean shopping at least once a week and patronizing stores and farmers' markets that offer good-quality organic produce. It also means storing food carefully and using it soon after the time of purchase, to keep it at its best.

That said, the New Healthy Kitchen is designed for real-life cooks with real-life schedules. Each recipe begins with a note on the amount of time needed to prepare and cook it, to help you figure out how to fit it into your day. And each chapter includes several "fresh ideas," simple dishes that are easy to pull together at the last minute.

You'll find that most of the recipes in this book are quick to make. Good-quality ingredients need less fussing over in the kitchen than mediocre ones. Steaming or roasting vegetables is not only healthy but also fast. A little vinaigrette is all that's needed to make a finished dish of many fresh raw vegetables. If your tomatoes are vine-ripened heirlooms, you don't need to do more than slice them and pass the olive oil and sea salt.

The simple act of cooking meals at home for ourselves and our families instead of loading up on take-out and restaurant food is a huge step toward healthy eating. The more frequently you shop and cook, the more of a habit it becomes, even in the midst of a busy day-to-day life. And the rewards are great. Eating meals at home is often the highlight of the day. It bonds couples and families together and makes us appreciate the good food around us. And no matter what recipes you use, your own cooking is bound to contain less butter, oil, and salt than restaurant food.

Eating by color helps to make us more conscious of presentation of the meal as a whole. Serve a starter that uses a green vegetable with a main course based on a red vegetable, for example. And follow a meat main dish graced with yellow or orange vegetables or fruit with a blue or purple fruit-based dessert. When finishing a dish, whether a starter, main dish, or dessert, don't forget the chef's trick of adding texture to a dish by topping soft, smooth foods with crunchy ingredients, like toasted walnuts sprinkled on a salad of pears and blue cheese. Combining colors, flavors, and textures in one meal adds to its appeal.

Portion size is another significant part of healthy eating. Make sure to limit proteins and fats, especially, to small portions. Rather than serving one starter followed by a main dish, you might choose to serve three starters in succession or at once, as a way to eat lightly and with more variety. Or, if you choose a starter featuring meat or cheese, you can follow it and balance it with a meatless main course.

The recipes in *Starters* have been chosen to give you a wide range of colors and ingredients to begin your meals. From vegetarian openers such as Yellow Beet and Yellow Pear Tomato Salad (page 86) to dishes for meat lovers such as Red Onion Marmalade and Pork Canapés (page 94), this book offers a variety of quick, fresh dishes that are the opening act for a colorful and healthy meal.

eggplants prunes blackberries

PURPLE AND BLUE FRUITS AND VEGETABLES PROMOTE

purple carrots black currants

MEMORY FUNCTION • HELP PROMOTE URINARY TRACT

lavender blue potatoes purple

HEALTH • BOOST THE IMMUNE SYSTEM • HELP PROMOTE

cabbage raisins black grapes

HEALTHY AGING • OFFER ANTIOXIDANTS FOR HEALING

purple figs blue plums purple

AND PROTECTION • HELP REDUCE THE RISK OF SOME

bell peppers purple asparagus

CANCERS • PURPLE AND BLUE FRUITS AND VEGETABLES

Purple & blue

Purple and blue fruits and vegetables are the exotics of the produce world. Like blue and purple flowers, they have a rare and special allure. They also rank high on the list of the most healthful foods. It's easy to add a splash of rich purple color to an otherwise everyday dish by including purple berries at the height of summer, or purple-tipped Belgian endive (chicory/witloof) in winter.

Blue and purple fruits and vegetables—especially the berries, such as blueberries and blackberries—are especially rich in antioxidants that protect the brain and memory. Other naturally healthful blue and purple fruits that are easily incorporated into daily cooking and eating include plums, purple grapes, and purple figs. Purple vegetables include the familiar purple eggplant, both the large globe and the long, slender Japanese, as well as purple (red) cabbage. Purple asparagus, bell peppers, and potatoes (sometimes called blue potatoes) are less common, but their unusual coloration adds both nutrients and drama to such dishes as Purple Asparagus Roasted with Prosciutto (page 34) and Warm Purple Potato Salad (page 24).

Raisins and prunes are available year-round and keep well on the pantry shelf. The process of drying intensifies the nutritional content of these fruits, making them an indispensable and delicious part of the healthy kitchen.

SPRING	SUMMER	AUTUMN	WINTER
purple asparagus	purple bell peppers	purple-tipped Belgian endive	purple-tipped Belgian endive
purple-tipped Belgian endive	blackberries	purple bell peppers	purple cabbage
blueberries	black currants	blueberries	purple carrots
purple cabbage	blueberries	purple cabbage	dried currants
purple carrots	eggplant	purple carrots	blue, purple, and black grapes
black currants	purple figs	dried currants	blue potatoes
dried currants	lavender	eggplant	prunes
prunes	blue, purple, and black plums	purple figs	raisins
raisins		blue, purple, and black grapes	
		blue, purple, and black plums	
		blue potatoes	
		prunes	
		raisins	

purple belgian endive & crab salad

Leaves from 2 heads purple-tipped Belgian endive (chicory/witloof) or regular Belgian endive

4 tsp rice wine vinegar

1 lb (500 g) fresh or thawed frozen lump crabmeat

1 Tbsp minced fresh tarragon

2 Tbsp extra-virgin olive oil

1 Tbsp mayonnaise

2 tsp capers, chopped

2 drops of Tabasco sauce

1 Tbsp lemon juice

Arrange 3 or 4 endive leaves on each of 4 chilled salad plates. Coarsely chop remaining leaves and make a bed of them on arranged leaves.

Combine vinegar, crabmeat, tarragon, olive oil, mayonnaise, capers, Tabasco, and lemon juice in a bowl and season with ½ tsp salt and ¼ tsp pepper. Divide the crab mixture equally among the plates, mounding it on the beds of chopped endive. Serve at once.

To prepare: 10 minutes

4 servings

blueberry salad

¼ cup (1 oz/30 g) chopped raw or blanched almonds

3 Tbsp extra-virgin olive oil

4 tsp raspberry vinegar

2 tsp minced shallot

1½ cups (6 oz/185 g) blueberries

1 Tbsp minced fresh chives

Leaves from 1 head butter (Boston) lettuce, torn into bite-sized pieces

½ cup (3 oz/90 g) crumbled feta cheese

Preheat oven to 300°F (150°C).

Put almonds on a baking sheet and bake until lightly golden, about 7 minutes. Remove from oven and set aside.

In a salad bowl, combine olive oil, vinegar, ¼ tsp salt, and ¼ tsp pepper and mix well. Add shallot, blueberries, and half of the chives. Let stand for 10–15 minutes.

Add butter lettuce and feta and toss well. Garnish with almonds and remaining chives, and serve at once.

To prepare: 25 minutes

To cook: 7 minutes

4 servings

italian-style grilled eggplant

⅓ cup (3 fl oz/80 ml) extra-virgin olive oil

2 globe eggplants (aubergines)

2 Tbsp minced fresh parsley

1 tsp fresh thyme

2 Tbsp balsamic vinegar

1 clove garlic, minced

Build a hot charcoal or wood fire in a grill or preheat a gas grill to 400°F (200°C). Rub grill grate with 1 tsp of olive oil.

Cut eggplants lengthwise into slices ½ inch (12 mm) thick. Brush both sides with olive oil and season with 1½ tsp salt and 1 tsp pepper. Grill until golden brown and crisp, 6–7 minutes. Turn and grill until golden brown and crisp on second side, about 4 minutes. Remove from grill and set aside.

Put remaining olive oil in a shallow baking dish with parsley, thyme, vinegar, and garlic. Add warm eggplant slices and let stand for 1 hour, then turn and let stand 1 hour more. Serve at once, or cover and refrigerate for up to 1 week. Serve at room temperature.

Note: Serve with Grilled Zucchini Skewers with Coriander (page 42) or Grilled Radicchio with Anchovy Sauce (page 99) for an antipasto platter.

To prepare: 20 minutes, plus 2 hours to stand

To cook: 15 minutes

4 servings

warm purple potato salad

2½ lb (1.25 kg) small purple potatoes

3 Tbsp extra-virgin olive oil

2 tsp red wine vinegar

¼ cup (1 oz/30 g) finely chopped celery

¼ cup (1 oz/30 g) finely chopped red onion

¼ cup (⅓ oz/10 g) minced fresh parsley

Put potatoes in a large pot and add cold water to cover by 3 inches (7.5 cm) and 1 tsp salt. Bring to a boil, then reduce heat to medium-low and cover. Simmer until tender, about 15 minutes. Drain and let cool to the touch. Peel and carefully cut into slices ¼ inch (6 mm) thick.

Combine potato slices, olive oil, and vinegar in a shallow bowl and turn gently to coat. Add celery, red onion, parsley, ½ tsp salt, and ½ tsp pepper. Gently stir until well mixed. Cover and let stand for 20 minutes at room temperature before serving.

To prepare: 20 minutes, plus 20 minutes to stand

To cook: 20 minutes

4 servings

roasted plums stuffed with blue cheese

4 purple plums, halved and pitted

2 tsp olive oil

3 oz (90 g) soft blue cheese, such as Gorgonzola, at room temperature

4–8 slices walnut or whole-grain bread

4 sprigs watercress

Preheat oven to 450°F (230°C).

Coat outside of plums with olive oil and mound a teaspoonful or so of cheese in each cavity. Place plums in a shallow baking dish just large enough to hold them and bake just until cheese has warmed through, about 10 minutes. Remove from oven and let cool.

Serve the plums on small plates, accompanied by walnut bread and garnished with watercress.

To prepare: 10 minutes

To cook: 10 minutes

4 servings

fresh fig & goat cheese salad

8 fresh purple figs, stemmed

2 tsp extra-virgin olive oil, plus 3 Tbsp

1 Tbsp red wine vinegar

2 cups (2 oz/60 g) mixed baby greens

3 oz (90 g) soft goat cheese, cut into 4 pieces

½ tsp balsamic vinegar

Coat figs with 2 tsp olive oil, then cut them lengthwise into quarters.

In a salad bowl, combine all but a few drops of the 3 Tbsp olive oil with red wine vinegar. Add ¼ tsp salt, ¼ tsp pepper, and baby greens and toss well to coat.

Divide dressed greens evenly among 4 salad plates. Arrange 8 fig quarters on each and top with a piece of goat cheese. Drizzle cheese with remaining olive oil and a drop or two of balsamic vinegar.

To prepare: 15 minutes

4 servings

purple grapes in salads

Purple grapes add not only flavor and nutrients to salads, but their color is also a beautiful contrast with greens. Add halved seedless purple grapes to a baby spinach or arugula (rocket) salad and top with crumbled blue cheese.

purple bell peppers & dip

Purple bell peppers (capsicums) make for an interesting crudité platter. Serve with feta cheese mashed with a little plain low-fat yogurt and seasoned with minced capers, minced fresh parsley and tarragon, salt, and pepper.

roasted stuffed figs

Rub whole or halved figs with a little olive oil before roasting. Roast in a 350°F (180°C) oven until plumped and warmed through. Sprinkle with crumbled fresh goat cheese, mint leaves, and pine nuts, and serve.

chicory salad with purple figs

Whisk olive oil and vinegar together in a salad bowl and add salt and pepper. Add raisins, currants, and torn chicory and toss. Roast quartered figs in a 350°F (180°C) oven. Add to salad with hazelnuts (filberts) and Gorgonzola and serve.

purple cabbage slaw with raisins

½ head purple or green cabbage

¼ white onion

¼ cup (1½ oz/45 g) raisins

¼ cup (2 fl oz/60 ml) mayonnaise

1 Tbsp red wine vinegar

2 Tbsp whole or low-fat milk

½ tsp sugar

Finely shred cabbage and onion. Soak raisins in warm water for about 10 minutes to soften. Drain and set aside.

Combine mayonnaise, vinegar, and milk in a small bowl; whisk with a fork to combine. Add sugar, and salt and pepper to taste (dressing should have a sweet/sour balance). Toss cabbage, onion, and raisins with dressing.

Serve at once on chilled salad plates or bowls.

To prepare: 20 minutes

4 servings

purple kale crostini

4 Tbsp (2 fl oz/60 ml) extra-virgin olive oil

2 Tbsp finely chopped onion

2 cloves garlic

1 lb (500 g) purple kale, tough stems removed, leaves coarsely chopped

1 cup (8 fl oz/250 ml) low-sodium chicken broth

12 baguette slices, ¼ inch (6 mm) thick, toasted

¼ cup (1 oz/30 g) shaved pecorino cheese

In a saucepan, heat 2 Tbsp olive oil over medium-high heat and sauté onion until translucent, about 2 minutes. Add garlic and kale and sauté until kale is limp, 3–4 minutes. Add chicken broth, reduce heat to low, cover, and cook until kale is tender, 10–15 minutes.

Remove kale from pan, let cool, and squeeze out liquid. In a bowl, stir together kale, ½ tsp salt, and ½ tsp pepper. Top each baguette slice with a little kale, a drizzle of olive oil, and some shaved cheese.

Preheat broiler (grill). Place baguette slices on a baking sheet about 6 inches (15 cm) from heat source and broil (grill) until cheese has just melted, about 3 minutes. Serve hot.

To prepare: 15 minutes

To cook: 25 minutes

4–6 servings

purple bell pepper & goat cheese terrine

4 oz (125 g) soft goat cheese at room temperature

2 Tbsp whole or low-fat milk

1 Tbsp minced shallot

1 purple bell pepper (capsicum)

Crackers for serving

Butter a 4–fl oz (125-ml) ramekin and line with a sheet of plastic wrap. Put goat cheese in a bowl and mash it with a fork. Stir in milk to make a thick spread. Stir in shallot, ½ tsp salt, and ¼ tsp pepper.

Seed and cut bell pepper into lengthwise strips ½ inch (12 mm) wide. Reserve 3 strips. Lay remaining pepper strips snugly side by side in bottom of ramekin to cover it. Gently pack in half of the cheese mixture. Mince reserved pepper strips and sprinkle them over the top to make a solid layer. Cover with remaining cheese, smoothing top. Refrigerate overnight to firm.

To serve, pull on ends of plastic to lift cheese from ramekin. Invert on a serving dish and peel off plastic. Surround with crackers to serve.

Note: Purple bell peppers have a flavor similar to that of green bell peppers. If you like, use other, sweeter colors of pepper for this dish: red, orange, or yellow.

To prepare: 30 minutes, plus chilling overnight

4 servings

eggplant pesto

1 globe eggplant (aubergine)

3 rounds pita bread, each cut into 8 triangles

2 cloves garlic, minced

½ cup (2 oz/60 g) chopped walnuts

2 cups (2 oz/60 g) packed fresh basil leaves

2–3 Tbsp extra-virgin olive oil

1 Tbsp capers, crushed

Preheat oven to 350°F (180°C). Place eggplant on a baking sheet and bake until slightly collapsed and tender inside, about 1 hour. Remove from oven and let cool to the touch. Leave oven on. Remove and discard skin, and coarsely chop flesh. Set aside.

Place pita triangles on another baking sheet and bake until lightly golden, about 15 minutes, turning once. Remove bread from oven and set aside.

In a blender, combine eggplant, garlic, 1 tsp salt, walnuts, basil, and 2 Tbsp olive oil. Purée. If too thick, add 1 Tbsp oil. Stir in capers. Serve with pita bread triangles.

To prepare: 15 minutes

To cook: 1 hour 15 minutes

4–6 servings (about 2 cups)

brie & smoked chicken with blueberry compote

3 dried juniper berries

1 Tbsp olive oil

1 Tbsp finely chopped onion

1½ cups (6 oz/185 g) fresh or frozen blueberries

2 Tbsp brandy or dry vermouth

½ cup (½ oz/15 g) baby arugula (rocket) leaves or other mild salad greens

6 oz (185 g) smoked chicken or duck breast, thinly sliced, any fat removed

3 oz (90 g) Brie cheese, thinly sliced

Grind juniper berries in a mortar with a pestle or in a spice mill.

Heat olive oil in a saucepan over medium heat and sauté onion until translucent, about 2 minutes. Add blueberries and ground juniper and cook, crushing blueberries with back of a wooden spoon until softened, about 5 minutes. Add brandy and simmer, stirring occasionally, until thickened, about 7 minutes. Stir in ¼ tsp salt. Remove from heat and let cool slightly.

Divide arugula leaves among 4 salad plates. Arrange slices of chicken and Brie on the arugula. Drizzle warm compote on top. Serve at once.

To prepare: 20 minutes

To cook: 15 minutes

4 servings

purple asparagus roasted with prosciutto

16 spears purple or green asparagus (about 1 lb/500 g)

2 Tbsp balsamic vinegar

2 Tbsp red wine vinegar

1 Tbsp extra-virgin olive oil

8 thin slices prosciutto, halved lengthwise

Preheat oven to 450°F (230°C).

Put asparagus spears in a baking dish in a single layer and sprinkle with ¼ tsp salt and ¼ tsp pepper. Pour vinegars and olive oil over and turn to coat. Wrap each spear with a half-slice of prosciutto. Return to baking dish, turning several times. Roast in oven, turning several times, until prosciutto is crisp and asparagus is tender-crisp, about 20 minutes. Serve hot or at room temperature.

To prepare: 10 minutes

To cook: 20 minutes

4 servings

avocados cucumbers spinach

GREEN FRUITS AND VEGETABLES BOOST THE IMMUNE

watercress arugula asparagus

SYSTEM • PROMOTE EYE HEALTH • HELP BUILD STRONG

kale broccoli snow peas leeks

BONES • BUILD STRONG TEETH • OFFER ANTIOXIDANTS

lettuce zucchini green beans

FOR HEALING AND PROTECTION • REDUCE THE RISK OF

endive brussels sprouts limes

CERTAIN CANCERS • GREEN FRUITS AND VEGETABLES

green tea kiwifruits artichokes

BOOST THE IMMUNE SYSTEM • PROMOTE EYE HEALTH

Green

Green is the broadest band in the colorful produce spectrum, with flavors and textures ranging from creamy avocados to cooling honeydews. We all know that it's healthy to eat our greens. In fact, the darker the leaves of the vegetable—think kale, chard, and spinach—the more packed with nutrients. And the recipes in this chapter make eating greens a pleasure rather than a chore.

Every season has its own green produce. Green apples abound in the autumn, while leafy greens like collards and kale keep us healthy through the cold winter. Fresh basil and other herbs tell us that summer is here, while spearlike asparagus and thorny artichokes filling up the market's produce aisle are harbingers of spring.

It's especially easy to include green vegetables in first courses, since salads are a classic opener to a meal. And when you combine traditional salad greens with another green vegetable or fruit, as in Celery and Turkey Salad (page 51), or pair two green vegetables in one starter, as in the Polenta Galettes with Leek and Swiss Chard (page 52), you've doubled up on servings of this beneficial color in just one course of a meal.

Green fruits can make a welcome appearance in savory starters, such as in Green Pears Baked with Stilton Cheese (page 48) and Kiwifruit, Apple, and Grape Salad with Rosemary Syrup (page 45).

SPRING	SUMMER	AUTUMN	WINTER
artichokes	arugula	green apples	green apples
asparagus	Hass avocados	artichokes	Fuerte avocados
green bell peppers	green beans	bok choy	bok choy
endive	green chiles	broccoli	broccoli
green beans	cucumbers	broccoli rabe	broccoli rabe
kiwifruits	green grapes	Brussels sprouts	Brussels sprouts
lettuce	green herbs	green cabbage	green cabbage
Persian and Key limes	Persian and Key limes	endive	celery
green pears	green-fleshed melons	green beans	endive
peas	okra	kale	kale
snow peas	sugar snap peas	leeks	leeks
sugar snap peas	spinach	green pears	snow peas
spinach	zucchini	Swiss chard	spinach
watercress		watercress	watercress

artichoke soup
with crostini

2½ lb (1.25 kg) baby artichokes

2 Tbsp plus 1 tsp olive oil

1 Tbsp finely chopped onion

1 clove garlic, minced

4 cups (32 fl oz/1 l) low-sodium chicken broth

1 bay leaf

1 tsp minced fresh thyme

1 lemon slice

1 tsp grated lemon zest

4 slices baguette or country-style bread

½ cup (2 oz/60 g) shredded Swiss or Gruyère cheese

Prepare artichokes (see page 45). Heat 2 Tbsp olive oil in a frying pan over medium-high heat. Add onion and sauté until translucent, about 2 minutes. Drain and pat artichokes dry and add to onion along with garlic. Sauté until color deepens, about 2 minutes. Add broth, bay leaf, thyme, and lemon slice. Bring to a boil, reduce heat to low, and cook until artichokes are fork-tender, about 15 minutes.

Remove lemon slice and bay leaf, and purée soup using an immersion or stand blender. Strain through a fine-mesh sieve. Return to a clean pan and heat to a rapid simmer over medium heat. Stir in lemon zest, ¼ tsp salt, and ¼ tsp pepper.

Preheat broiler (grill). Brush one side of bread slices with 1 tsp olive oil, place on a baking sheet about 6 inches (15 cm) from heat source, and broil (grill) until lightly golden, about 3 minutes. Turn and broil second side, 1–2 minutes. Remove from broiler and top each toast with some cheese. Return to broiler until cheese has melted, about 2 minutes. Ladle hot soup into warmed bowls and garnish with the crostini. Grind fresh pepper on top and serve.

To prepare: 25 minutes

To cook: 30 minutes

4 servings

cucumber & feta
cheese salad

2 cucumbers, peeled and thinly sliced

½ red onion, finely chopped

2 Tbsp minced fresh dill

4 tsp rice wine vinegar

2 Tbsp extra-virgin olive oil

¾ cup (4 oz/125 g) crumbled feta cheese

Make a layer of half the cucumber slices in a bowl. Sprinkle with half of the onion, half of the dill, ¼ tsp salt, and ¼ tsp pepper. Repeat to make another layer. Pour vinegar and olive oil over and let stand for 30 minutes to meld flavors. Stir to combine, then add feta cheese and toss gently.

Serve in chilled salad bowls.

To prepare: 10 minutes, plus 30 minutes to stand

4 servings

grilled zucchini skewers with coriander

4 zucchini (courgettes), cut crosswise into slices ½ inch (12 mm) thick

2 Tbsp olive oil

1 tsp dried oregano

1 tsp coriander seeds, crushed

½ tsp mild chili powder

1 cup (8 oz/250 g) plain whole or low-fat yogurt

1 tsp ground cumin

¼ tsp cayenne pepper

Cilantro sprigs for garnish

Soak 8 wooden skewers in water to cover for 30 minutes. Set aside.

Build a hot charcoal or wood fire in a grill or preheat a gas grill to 400°F (200°C). In a bowl, combine zucchini slices with oil, oregano, coriander, chili powder, and 1 tsp salt. Turn to coat and let stand for 30 minutes.

Thread zucchini sideways onto skewers. Grill 5–6 minutes on one side, or until lightly browned, then turn and cook second side until lightly browned and tender, 4–5 minutes. Brush with more marinade if desired.

In a bowl, mix together yogurt, cumin, cayenne, and ¼ teaspoon salt. Serve skewers with yogurt alongside, garnished with cilantro sprigs.

To prepare: 15 minutes, plus 30 minutes to stand

To cook: 10 minutes

4 servings

avocado, grapefruit & chive salad

2 Tbsp shelled pumpkin seeds

3 Tbsp extra-virgin olive oil

2 tsp raspberry vinegar

1 tsp honey

Leaves from 1 head green-leaf lettuce, torn into bite-sized pieces

2 white or pink grapefruits, peeled and segmented (see page 103)

2 thin slices red onion, separated into rings

2 avocados, peeled and pitted

2 Tbsp minced fresh chives

Preheat oven to 350°F (180°C).

Place pumpkin seeds on a baking sheet and toast in oven, shaking once or twice, until golden brown, about 7 minutes.

In a salad bowl, whisk together olive oil, vinegar, honey, ¼ tsp salt, and ¼ tsp pepper. Add lettuce.

Cut each grapefruit segment into 2 or 3 pieces, removing any seeds, and add to salad bowl along with red onion. Toss until well coated with dressing. Divide equally among 4 salad plates. Cube avocados and divide equally among salad plates.

Serve at once, sprinkled with chives and pumpkin seeds.

To prepare: 20 minutes

To cook: 7 minutes

4 servings

kiwifruit, apple & grape salad with rosemary syrup

¼ cup (2 oz/60 g) sugar

Three 6-inch (15-cm) stems rosemary

3 kiwifruits, peeled and diced

2 unpeeled tart green apples such as Granny Smith, cored and cut into ½-inch (12-mm) dice

1 cup (6 oz/185 g) seedless green grapes

Bring sugar and ½ cup (4 fl oz/125 ml) water to a boil in a saucepan over medium-high heat, stirring to dissolve sugar. Add rosemary stems, reduce heat to medium, and cook for 15 minutes. Remove rosemary and raise heat to high. Cook, stirring, until liquid is reduced to about ⅓ cup (3 fl oz/80 ml). Let cool to room temperature.

Put diced kiwis, diced apples, and grapes in a bowl and pour syrup over, tossing to coat fruit. Serve at once.

To prepare: 30 minutes

To cook: 20 minutes

4 servings

baby artichokes with black olives & lemon

4 rounds pita bread

1 lemon

12–15 baby artichokes

2 Tbsp extra-virgin olive oil

2 tsp minced fresh parsley

2 tsp fresh thyme leaves

20–25 oil-cured black olives, pitted

Preheat oven to 350°F (180°C). Cut each pita bread round into 8 triangles. Place on a baking sheet and bake until crisp, about 15 minutes, turning once. Remove from oven and set aside.

Grate all zest from lemon and set aside. Cut lemon in half and squeeze juice of one half into a large bowl of cold water.

Break off and discard leaves of each artichoke, leaving pale green leaves. Cut off upper third of artichokes. Trim stem end and rough edges where leaves were broken off. Cut artichokes in half or into quarters, depending on size. Cut off any purple interior tips. Place cut artichokes in bowl of lemon water.

Fill a large saucepan halfway with water and squeeze about 1 Tbsp of lemon juice from remaining lemon half into it. Bring to a boil and add artichokes. Cook until barely fork-tender, 3–4 minutes. Drain well. While still warm, place artichokes in a bowl with olive oil, ½ tsp salt, ½ tsp pepper, parsley, thyme, and olives. Sprinkle with lemon zest and toss well. Serve in bowls, accompanied with pita triangles.

To prepare: 25 minutes

To cook: 20 minutes

4 servings

edamame

In a covered steamer set over gently simmering water, steam fresh or frozen edamame (soy bean) pods until beans inside are tender, about 15 minutes. Serve beans in their pods, sprinkled with coarse salt. Pop beans from pods to eat.

frozen green grapes with cilantro

Freeze green grapes until they are hard. Serve in dessert bowls or old-fashioned Champagne saucers, garnished with minced cilantro (fresh coriander) and sprinkled with dry sherry.

kiwifruit salad

Peel and slice kiwifruits and toss with
torn leaves of butter (Boston) lettuce.
Scatter with arugula (rocket) leaves,
then drizzle with extra-virgin olive oil,
champagne vinegar, and lemon juice.
Sprinkle with chopped pistachios.

green pears
with serrano ham

Stem, halve, and core green pears, such
as Anjou, Comice, or Seckel. Cut into
wedges and wrap each wedge in serrano
ham or prosciutto. Offer toasted walnut
halves alongside.

green pears baked with stilton cheese

1 tsp butter, plus 1 Tbsp, melted

2 green pears, such as Anjou or Comice, halved and cored

1 Tbsp lemon juice

¼ cup (2 oz/60 g) Stilton cheese at room temperature

Watercress sprigs or arugula (rocket) leaves for garnish (optional)

Preheat oven to 350°F (180°C).

With 1 tsp butter, grease a baking dish just large enough to hold pears. Place pear halves in dish, cut side up, and drizzle with lemon juice. Fill cavity of each pear half with 1 mounded Tbsp cheese.

Bake pears for 15 minutes, then brush with melted butter and bake until fork-tender, about 10 more minutes. Serve warm, garnished with watercress, if using.

To prepare: 10 minutes

To cook: 25 minutes

4 servings

open-face sandwiches with mint cream cheese

4 oz (125 g) whole or low-fat cream cheese at room temperature

½ tsp white pepper

2 Tbsp whole or low-fat milk

½ cup (½ oz/15 g) packed fresh mint leaves, minced, plus sprigs for garnish

2 Tbsp minced shallots

4–6 thin slices dark rye bread

1 cucumber, peeled and thinly sliced

Combine cream cheese and white pepper in a bowl and mash with back of a fork. Stir in milk to make a spreadable paste. Stir in minced mint and shallots until well blended.

Spread each piece of bread with cream cheese mixture, then top with overlapping cucumber slices. With a sharp knife, cut each sandwich in half on the diagonal and garnish with a mint sprig.

To prepare: 20 minutes

4–6 servings (8–12 half-sandwiches)

tuna rounds with tomatillo guacamole

1 ahi tuna loin, about 1 lb (500 g) and 2 inches (5 cm) in diameter

1 Tbsp olive oil

Guacamole

2 tomatillos

2 avocados

2 tsp minced shallot

1 Tbsp lime juice

Bring tuna to room temperature. Season all over with ½ tsp coarse salt and ½ tsp pepper. In a frying pan, heat olive oil over high heat until smoking. Add tuna and sear on all sides until browned, about 6 minutes. Remove from pan and let rest.

For Guacamole: Rinse, husk, and finely chop tomatillos. Peel, pit, and mash avocados and stir in tomatillos and shallot. Season with ½ tsp salt, ½ tsp pepper, and lime juice.

Slice tuna loin to desired thickness, top with a spoonful of guacamole, and serve.

To prepare: 15 minutes

To cook: 10 minutes

6–8 servings

celery & turkey salad

2 cups (12 oz/375 g) finely chopped celery (about 4 stalks)

2 cups (12 oz/375 g) coarsely chopped cooked turkey

¼ cup (⅓ oz/10 g) minced fresh parsley

1 green (spring) onion, minced

1 Tbsp dried cranberries

¼ cup (2 oz/60 g) plain low-fat yogurt

2 Tbsp mayonnaise

4 large leaves butter (Boston) lettuce

Combine celery, turkey, parsley, green onion, cranberries, yogurt, and mayonnaise in a bowl and mix well. Season with 1 tsp salt and 1 tsp pepper. Mix again and let stand at room temperature for 30 minutes or refrigerate for up to 3 hours for flavors to meld.

To serve, place a lettuce leaf on each of 4 salad plates and arrange the salad on each leaf.

Note: This salad is excellent as a sandwich spread.

To prepare: 15 minutes, plus 30 minutes to 3 hours to chill

4 servings (12 canapés)

polenta galettes with leek & swiss chard

1 bunch Swiss chard, tough stems removed, coarsely chopped

1 cup (7 oz/220 g) fine- or medium-grind polenta

1 Tbsp butter

3 Tbsp extra-virgin olive oil

2 Tbsp minced shallots

4 cups (1 lb/500 kg) chopped leeks, white and pale green parts only (about 6 leeks)

⅓ cup (3 fl oz/80 ml) low-sodium chicken broth

½ tsp red pepper flakes

⅓ cup (1½ oz/45 g) shredded Gruyère cheese

Combine chard with 1 cup (8 fl oz/250 ml) water in a saucepan and bring to a boil over medium-high heat. Reduce heat to low, cover, and simmer until tender, about 15 minutes. Drain and set aside.

Combine 4 cups (32 fl oz/1 l) water and 1½ tsp kosher salt in a saucepan and bring to a boil over medium-high heat. Gradually stir in polenta, reduce heat to low, and simmer, stirring often, until polenta pulls slightly away from sides of pan, about 10 minutes. Butter a 10 x 14–inch (25 x 35–cm) baking pan, add polenta, and smooth top. Refrigerate for 30 minutes or until firm.

Melt butter with 2 Tbsp of olive oil in a frying pan over medium heat. Stir in shallots and leeks. Cover, reduce heat to low, and cook until leeks are very soft but not browned and moisture is completely absorbed, about 15 minutes. Stir in chard, chicken broth, red pepper flakes, 1 tsp salt, and ½ tsp black pepper. Raise heat to high and cook until almost all moisture is absorbed, about 5 minutes.

Preheat broiler (grill). Cut polenta into desired shapes, such as rectangles, circles, or triangles. Drizzle ½ Tbsp olive oil onto a baking sheet and place polenta cut-outs on it. Drizzle with remaining ½ Tbsp olive oil and sprinkle with half of the cheese. Broil (grill) 6 inches (15 cm) from heat source until lightly golden and cheese has melted, about 5 minutes. Divide polenta among warmed plates and top with some leek mixture. Sprinkle with remaining cheese and serve at once.

To prepare: 30 minutes

To cook: 50 minutes

4–6 servings

cauliflower shallots mushrooms

WHITE AND TAN FRUITS AND VEGETABLES CONTAIN

dates turnips bananas tan figs

ANTIOXIDANTS FOR HEALING AND PROTECTION • HELP

tan pears parsnips white corn

MAINTAIN A HEALTHY CHOLESTEROL LEVEL • PROMOTE

potatoes jerusalem artichokes

HEART HEALTH • BOOST THE IMMUNE SYSTEM • SLOW

ginger kohlrabi white peaches

CHOLESTEROL ABSORPTION • WHITE AND TAN FRUITS

garlic white nectarines jicama

AND VEGETABLES OFFER ANTIOXIDANTS FOR HEALING

White & tan

For all the emphasis on color in this book, it's important to remember that paler white and tan produce also has its place in the diet. White potatoes, which are often thought of as just a carbohydrate, are rich in vitamins and minerals, while onions and garlic add incomparable flavor as well as nutrients to many dishes. Sweet fruits such as dates and tan figs are also included in this category.

White and tan vegetables, such as jicama, cauliflower, white corn, celery root (celeriac), and Jerusalem artichokes, not only add another hue to the food palette, making them important for color contrast on the plate, but are also important additions to the healthy kitchen. Sweet white corn is a special treat of summer, while cauliflower and celery root bring hearty flavor to the stews and casseroles of fall and winter.

The range of culinary uses for white and tan vegetables is wide and varied, from zesty Jicama and Shrimp Ceviche (page 66) to Mushrooms Stuffed with Serrano Ham (page 59). A simple dish of Jerusalem Artichoke Soup with Truffle Oil (page 60) can be the understated opener for a vibrantly colored main course. And don't forget white and tan fruits such as bananas (whose inedible skins are yellow, but whose creamy flesh is white), tan pears, and white nectarines and peaches; their subtle colors and flavors add visual interest to dishes like White Nectarine and Mint Salad (page 64).

SPRING	SUMMER	AUTUMN	WINTER
bananas	bananas	bananas	cauliflower
cauliflower	white corn	cauliflower	dates
dates	dates	dates	garlic
garlic	tan figs	tan figs	ginger
ginger	garlic	Jerusalem artichokes	Jerusalem artichokes
jicama	ginger	jicama	jicama
mushrooms	kohlrabi	kohlrabi	dried mushrooms
onions	mushrooms	mushrooms	onions
parsnips	white nectarines	onions	parsnips
tan pears	onions	parsnips	tan pears
potatoes	white peaches	tan pears	potatoes
shallots	tan pears	potatoes	shallots
turnips	potatoes	shallots	turnips
	shallots	turnips	

mushrooms stuffed with serrano ham

20 button or cremini mushrooms

5 or 6 thin slices serrano ham or prosciutto

4 Tbsp (2 fl oz/60 ml) olive oil

2 Tbsp minced shallots

¼ cup (½ oz/15 g) fresh bread crumbs

3 Tbsp minced fresh parsley

2 Tbsp capers, minced

¼ cup (1 oz/30 g) grated Parmesan cheese

Preheat oven to 375°F (190°C). Remove stems from mushrooms. Mince stems and set aside with whole caps. Mince 5 slices ham. Cut remaining slice into thin strips for garnish, if desired.

Heat 2 Tbsp of olive oil in a frying pan over medium-high heat. Add shallots and sauté until soft, about 1 minute. Add mushroom stems and sauté for 1–2 minutes, then add minced ham, bread crumbs, parsley, and capers.

Put mushroom caps in a bowl and toss with 1 Tbsp olive oil. Fill each cap with crumb filling and place in a baking dish just large enough to hold them. Top with cheese and drizzle with remaining olive oil. Bake until mushrooms are tender and cheese is melted, about 15 minutes. Serve warm, garnished with ham strips, if using.

To prepare: 20 minutes

To cook: 20 minutes

6–8 servings
(20 mushrooms)

tan pear, walnut & blue cheese salad

2 Tbsp lemon juice

2 Tbsp walnut oil

4 leaves butter (Boston) lettuce

2 unpeeled tan pears, such as Bosc or Asian, halved, stemmed, and cored

2–3 oz (60–90 g) blue cheese

4 walnut halves, plus ¼ cup (1 oz/ 30 g) chopped walnuts, toasted (see page 121)

Combine lemon juice, walnut oil, and ½ tsp salt together in a small bowl and mix well to make dressing.

Lay a lettuce leaf on each of 4 salad plates. Place each pear half, flesh side up, on a cutting board and cut thin lengthwise slices three-quarters of the way through. Place a sliced pear half on each lettuce leaf, cut side up. Divide the cheese equally among pears, putting a nugget of cheese in each pear cavity. Top with a walnut half, and then sprinkle with some chopped walnuts. Drizzle with a little dressing and serve.

To prepare: 15 minutes

4 servings

jerusalem artichoke soup with truffle oil

1 lb (500 g) Jerusalem artichokes (sunchokes), peeled and coarsely chopped

3 cups (24 fl oz/750 ml) low-sodium chicken broth

½ tsp white pepper

2 tsp white truffle oil

Combine Jerusalem artichokes and chicken broth in a saucepan and bring to a boil. Reduce heat to low and simmer until vegetables are tender, about 15 minutes.

Purée using an immersion or stand blender. Add white pepper and ½ tsp salt. Return soup to a simmer. Ladle hot soup into warmed bowls and drizzle each with ½ tsp truffle oil. Serve at once.

To prepare: 20 minutes

To cook: 20 minutes

4 servings

mediterranean salad with roasted garlic dressing

2 heads garlic

5 Tbsp (2½ fl oz/75 ml) extra-virgin olive oil, plus more for drizzling

1 globe eggplant (aubergine)

2 red bell peppers (capsicums)

1 zucchini (courgette)

2 Tbsp red wine vinegar

¼ cup (⅓ oz/10 g) chopped fresh basil for garnish

¼ cup (1 oz/30 g) pine nuts, toasted (see page 121) for garnish

Preheat oven to 350°F (180°C).

Cut about ½ inch (12 mm) off top of each garlic head. Drizzle each with a little olive oil, wrap in foil, and place on a baking sheet. Bake until soft, about 45 minutes. Let cool, then squeeze garlic from cloves into a bowl. Set aside. Raise oven temperature to 400°F (200°C).

Meanwhile, cut eggplant into ½-inch (12-mm) dice and peppers into ½-inch (12-mm) squares. Cut zucchini into slices ½ inch (12 mm) thick. Combine vegetables in a bowl and add 3 tablespoons olive oil, ¼ tsp salt, and ¼ tsp pepper. Toss to coat well. Spread on an oiled baking sheet and bake, shaking once or twice, until golden, 15–20 minutes. Remove from oven and let cool.

Add remaining 1½ Tbsp olive oil, ¼ tsp salt, ¼ tsp pepper, and vinegar to roasted garlic. Mash and mix lightly with a fork, leaving some garlic in chunks.

Put vegetables in a bowl or on a platter and pour dressing over, turning to coat. Garnish with basil and pine nuts.

To prepare: 20 minutes

To cook: 1 hour 5 minutes

4 servings

caramelized onion & shallot pissaladière

Dough

1 cup (8 fl oz/250 ml) warm water (about 105°F/40°C)

1 package (2¼ teaspoons) active dry yeast

1 tsp sugar

1 tsp salt

2 Tbsp olive oil

3–3½ cups (15–17½ oz/470–545 g) unbleached all-purpose (plain) flour

Topping

4 Tbsp (2 oz/60 g) butter

6 Tbsp (3 fl oz/90 ml) olive oil

3 lb (1.5 kg) onions, very thinly sliced

2 lb (1 kg) shallots, very thinly sliced

1 Tbsp sugar

2 Tbsp dry white wine

Cornmeal for sprinkling

2 Tbsp extra-virgin olive oil

1 Tbsp dried oregano

¼ cup (1 oz/30 g) grated Parmesan cheese

12 pitted Niçoise olives

For dough: Put warm water in a small bowl and stir in yeast and sugar. Let stand until foamy, 5 minutes. Transfer to a food processor, add salt, olive oil, and 3 cups flour. Process until a ball forms, 2–3 minutes. If dough is too sticky, add a little more flour. Alternatively, mix in a stand mixer or in a bowl with a wooden spoon.

Place dough on a floured surface and knead until smooth and elastic, about 7 minutes. Put dough in an oiled bowl, turn to coat, and cover with a damp towel. Let rise in a warm place until doubled, about 1½ hours.

For topping: Melt butter with olive oil in a large, heavy saucepan over medium heat. Add half of the onions and shallots. Sprinkle with half of the sugar and ½ tsp salt. Add remaining onions and shallots, remaining sugar, and another ½ tsp salt. Cover, reduce heat to low, and cook until vegetables have softened and begun to release their moisture, about 20 minutes. Uncover, raise heat to medium, and stir. Cook, stirring occasionally, until vegetables begin to turn golden and become very soft, about 15 minutes. Raise heat to high and cook, stirring often, until a deep golden brown, about 10 minutes. Add wine and stir to scrape up browned bits, then cook until wine has evaporated, about 5 minutes.

Preheat oven to 500°F (260°C). Punch down dough and let rest for 15 minutes. Transfer to floured surface, flatten with your hands, and roll out to a 14 x 18–inch (35 x 45–cm) rectangle. Sprinkle a pan of same size with cornmeal and lay dough in it, pressing it over pan rim. Drizzle with 1 Tbsp olive oil. Spread topping evenly over dough. Bake until rim is golden and crisp, 12–15 minutes. Remove from oven and sprinkle with oregano and remaining olive oil. Top with Parmesan cheese and olives. Serve hot or at room temperature, cut into squares.

To prepare: 2½ hours

To cook: 65 minutes

8–12 servings

white nectarine & mint salad

Cut nectarines into thin slices and place them in a bowl. Sprinkle with lemon juice, minced fresh mint, and honey. Toss to blend and let stand at room temperature for about 5 minutes. Serve in small bowls, garnished with mint sprigs.

broiled portobellos

Toss portobello mushrooms with olive oil, minced garlic, and minced parsley. Broil (grill), gill side up, until browned, about 4 minutes. Turn and broil other side for 1 minute. Cut into chunks and toss with mâche leaves and Parmesan shavings.

raisin-date spread on rye

Make a spread of chopped dates and finely chopped golden raisins (sultanas) with just enough cream cheese to hold it together. Add milk if needed for smoothness. Cover triangles of rye bread with spread and garnish with a date half.

jicama salad

Peel jicama with a paring knife or vegetable peeler and cut into thin strips. Drizzle with a small amount of lime juice, top with crumbled feta cheese, and sprinkle with chili powder to taste. Toss to coat before serving.

jicama & shrimp ceviche

½ lb (250 g) shrimp (prawns), peeled

½ cup (4 fl oz/125 ml) lime juice (from about 8 limes)

2 cups (8 oz/250 g) peeled and diced jicama

¼ cup (⅓ oz/10 g) minced cilantro (fresh coriander)

2 Tbsp minced red onion

1 or 2 serrano chiles, seeded and minced

Tortilla chips for serving

In a bowl, combine shrimp and half of the lime juice and let stand, turning often, until shrimp is opaque, about 15–20 minutes. Remove to a board and coarsely chop shrimp.

Put chopped shrimp in a bowl with remaining lime juice, jicama, cilantro, onion, chiles, and ½ tsp salt. Toss well.

Divide among 4 chilled plates and accompany with tortilla chips.

To prepare: 30 minutes

4 servings

sherried mushroom soup

1 Tbsp butter

1 Tbsp minced shallot

1 Tbsp crumbled dried porcini mushroom

¼ cup (2 fl oz/60 ml) dry sherry, plus 2 tsp

4 cups (32 fl oz/1 l) low-sodium beef broth

1 lb (500 g) white button mushrooms, thinly sliced

1 tsp minced fresh thyme

1 Tbsp minced fresh parsley

In a saucepan, melt butter over medium heat and sauté shallot until translucent, about 1 minute. Add porcini, ¼ cup sherry, and 1 cup (8 fl oz/ 250 ml) beef broth. Bring to a boil over medium-high heat. Reduce heat to medium-low and simmer until reduced to ⅓ cup (3 fl oz/80 ml), about 30 minutes.

Strain through a fine-mesh sieve into a clean saucepan and discard porcini and shallot. Add ⅔ cup (5 fl oz/160 ml) water, remaining broth, and ¼ tsp salt to pan and bring to a boil. Reduce heat to low and simmer for 5 minutes. Reserve 12 of the best-looking fresh mushroom slices for garnish. Add remaining mushrooms to broth and simmer for 10 minutes. Stir in 2 tsp sherry and thyme. Taste and adjust seasoning.

Ladle hot soup into warmed bowls and garnish each with 3 mushroom slices and a sprinkle of parsley. Serve at once.

To prepare: 15 minutes

To cook: 55 minutes

4 servings

white corn pancakes with crème fraîche

Kernels cut from 4 ears white corn

¼ cup (1 oz/30 g) minced shallots

1 cup (5 oz/155 g) all-purpose (plain) flour

2 eggs, beaten

¼ cup (2 oz/60 g) crème fraîche, plus more for topping

3 tsp butter

2 Tbsp extra-virgin olive oil

Snipped fresh chives for garnish

In a bowl, combine corn kernels, shallots, flour, eggs, crème fraîche, ½ tsp salt, and ½ tsp pepper. Whisk well to blend.

Melt 1 tsp butter with 1 Tbsp olive oil in a frying pan over medium-high heat. Drop heaping tablespoonfuls of batter into pan 2½ inches (6 cm) apart. Press each to a scant ½ inch (12 mm) thick with a metal spatula. Fry until golden brown, 3–4 minutes on each side. Transfer to paper towels to drain, then keep warm in a low (150°F/65°C) oven. Repeat with remaining batter, adding butter and oil as needed and reducing heat to medium if browning too quickly.

Serve at once, topped with crème fraîche and sprinkled with chives.

To prepare: 15 minutes

To cook: 30 minutes

6 servings (18 pancakes)

crostini with tan figs & camembert cheese

6 oz (185 g) Camembert cheese

6–8 tan or brown figs, such as turkey, Kalmyrna, or Brunswick

12 thin slices baguette

1 Tbsp minced fresh thyme

Cut Camembert into thin slices and let sit at room temperature for 30 minutes. Stem figs and cut lengthwise into thin slices. Toast baguette slices in a toaster, or on a baking sheet in a preheated 350°F (180°C) oven until golden, about 5 minutes. Remove from oven and let cool.

Lay a slice or two of cheese on each baguette slice, spreading cheese with a knife. Top each with several slices of fig and sprinkle with thyme. Serve at room temperature.

To prepare: 35 minutes

To cook: 8 minutes

4 servings (12 crostini)

grapefruit papayas pineapples

YELLOW AND ORANGE FRUITS AND VEGETABLES HELP

apricots yellow pears pumpkins

PROMOTE HEART HEALTH • HELP REDUCE THE RISK OF

persimmons peaches kumquats

CERTAIN CANCERS • PROMOTE EYE HEALTH • CONTAIN

rutabagas golden beets carrots

ANTIOXIDANTS FOR HEALING AND PROTECTION • BOOST

yellow apples golden kiwifruits

THE IMMUNE SYSTEM • YELLOW AND ORANGE FRUITS

lemons navel oranges mangoes

AND VEGETABLES OFFER ANTIOXIDANTS FOR HEALING

Yellow & orange

Carrots, of course, are the classic "healthy" vegetable because of their well-documented role as a contributor to good vision. But many other members of the yellow and orange group of fruits and vegetables, including sweet potatoes, summer squashes, and citrus fruits, also offer essential vitamins, minerals, and antioxidants, in addition to an eye-pleasing, jewel-like presence on the plate.

This large group of the fruit-and-vegetable rainbow includes familiar oranges and yellow apples as well as more unusual golden beets and persimmons. And you can dine from this group in every season, feasting on yellow corn in summer, succulent pears in autumn, and velvety winter squash in the cold months.

The members of this color group are high in nutrients as well as flavor, bringing their intensity to starters like Yellow Beet and Yellow Pear Tomato Salad (page 86), Carrot Soup with Fresh Ginger (page 75), and Peach and Prosciutto Bruschetta (page 76). Try Persimmon and Yellow Apple Salad (page 76) to brighten a winter meal, or Corn Flans

with Lobster Topping (page 79) to open a summer dinner party.

The glorious colors of this group make them a welcome addition to salads in particular: Yellow grapefruit with green pistachios make a pleasing combination, and sliced kumquat adds flair to a salad of tender lettuce and sprightly herbs.

SPRING	SUMMER	AUTUMN	WINTER
carrots	apricots	yellow apples	yellow apples
grapefruit	yellow bell peppers	dried apricots	dried apricots
golden kiwifruit	corn	golden beets	golden beets
kumquats	mangoes	yellow bell peppers	carrots
lemons	orange melons	lemons	grapefruit
mangoes	nectarines	navel and mandarin oranges	kumquats
navel and mandarin oranges	Valencia oranges	yellow pears	lemons
papayas	papayas	persimmons	navel and mandarin oranges
pineapples	peaches	yellow potatoes	yellow pears
yellow potatoes	pineapples	pumpkins	yellow potatoes
sweet potatoes	golden raspberries	rutabagas	pumpkins
	yellow summer squash	orange winter squash	rutabagas
	yellow tomatoes	sweet potatoes	orange winter squash
			sweet potatoes

carrot soup with fresh ginger

2 tsp extra-virgin olive oil, plus 1 Tbsp

1 Tbsp grated orange zest

1 tsp thinly sliced fresh ginger

2 Tbsp minced shallots

1 lb (500 g) carrots, peeled and cut into 1-inch (2.5-cm) pieces

2 cups (16 fl oz/500 ml) low-sodium chicken broth

In a small bowl, stir 2 tsp olive oil and orange zest together. Set aside.

Heat remaining 1 Tbsp oil in a saucepan over medium heat. Add ginger and sauté until golden brown, about 2 minutes. Remove with a slotted spoon and set aside. Add shallots and sauté until translucent, about 2 minutes. Stir in carrots, then slowly add chicken broth, stirring well. Stir in ½ tsp salt. Bring to a boil, reduce heat to medium, cover, and simmer until carrots are fork-tender, 20–25 minutes.

Remove to a blender and purée until smooth. Add 1 tsp pepper. Taste and adjust seasoning. Return purée to saucepan. Heat over medium-high heat. Divide among warmed soup bowls. Drizzle ½ tsp orange-infused olive oil over each bowl and garnish with ¼ tsp sautéed ginger.

To prepare: 10 minutes

To cook: 35 minutes

4 servings

cantaloupe & feta cheese salad

2 cantaloupes

¼ cup (⅓ oz/10 g) minced cilantro (fresh coriander), plus sprigs for garnish

¼ cup (2 fl oz/60 ml) lime juice

½ cup (2½ oz/75 g) crumbled feta cheese

2 tsp chipotle or other chile powder

Cut each cantaloupe in half lengthwise and scoop out seeds with a large spoon. Cut each half into wedges 1 inch (2.5 cm) thick and remove rind.

Arrange cantaloupe slices on a serving platter, sprinkle with minced cilantro, and drizzle with lime juice. Sprinkle with feta cheese and chile powder. Garnish with cilantro sprigs and serve.

To prepare: 15 minutes

4–6 servings

persimmon & yellow apple salad

2 Fuyu persimmons

2 unpeeled yellow apples such as Golden Delicious

2 tsp lemon juice

2 Tbsp finely ground walnuts

1½ Tbsp sherry wine vinegar

2 Tbsp walnut oil or extra-virgin olive oil

¼ tsp sugar

Cut persimmons in half lengthwise, scoop out any seeds with a spoon, and cut halves into ½-inch (12-mm) cubes. Core apples with an apple corer or a small, sharp knife and cut into slices ¼ inch (6 mm) thick.

Combine persimmon cubes and apple slices in a bowl and drizzle with lemon juice. Toss well, then set aside.

In a large bowl, combine ground walnuts, vinegar, oil, ½ tsp salt, ¼ tsp pepper, and sugar. Stir to blend well. Add persimmons and apples to bowl and toss.

Serve at once on chilled salad plates.

To prepare: 10 minutes

4 servings

peach & prosciutto bruschetta

8 slices baguette

1 Tbsp olive oil

3 peaches

4 thin prosciutto slices, halved lengthwise

Preheat oven to 350°F (180°C).

Brush both sides of baguette slices with olive oil and place on a baking sheet. Bake until lightly golden, about 5 minutes, then turn and bake on second side until lightly golden, about 3 minutes. Remove from oven and set aside.

Dip peaches in boiling water for 30 seconds. Slip off skins. Cut in half and remove pit. Using a very sharp knife, cut peaches into thin slices. Arrange peach slices in a snug single layer on each toast. Rumple a half-slice of prosciutto on top of each and serve.

To prepare: 15 minutes

To cook: 8 minutes

6–8 servings (8 slices)

corn flans with lobster topping

1 lobster tail, thawed if frozen

2 slices bacon

½ onion, finely chopped

1 stalk celery, finely chopped

2¼ cups (18 fl oz/560 ml) whole or low-fat milk

Kernels cut from 3 ears yellow corn, cobs reserved

4 eggs

Fresh dill for garnish

To prepare: 40 minutes

To cook: 1 hour 10 minutes, plus 10 minutes to stand

4 servings

Cook lobster in a large saucepan of boiling water until meat is just opaque throughout, about 15 minutes. Transfer to a bowl of ice water for 10 minutes. Remove shell, reserving it. Cut meat crosswise into thin rounds. Reserve 4 of the most attractive rounds and chop remainder. Set aside.

Preheat oven to 325°F (165°C). In a large saucepan, cook bacon over medium heat to render its fat, about 5 minutes. Using a slotted spoon, remove bacon (keep for another use). Add onion and celery to the bacon fat and sauté until translucent, about 2 minutes. Add milk, reserved corn cobs, reserved lobster shell, 1 tsp salt, and ½ tsp pepper. Cover, reduce heat to medium-low, and simmer for 15 minutes. Remove lobster shell and corn cobs. Stir in corn kernels, raise heat to medium, and cook for 5 minutes. Use an immersion or stand blender to coarsely purée. Whisk eggs in a large bowl just to blend. Gradually whisk in hot milk mixture.

Butter four 6–fl oz (180-ml) ramekins. Place in a roasting pan and fill ramekins to within ½ inch (12 mm) of rims with flan mixture. Place pan in preheated oven and pour very hot (but not boiling) water into pan to reach halfway up sides of ramekins. Bake until only very center of flans trembles when shaken or tilted, about 40 minutes. Remove from oven and let flans stand in hot water for 10 minutes. Remove from hot water and run a knife around edges of each flan to loosen.

Place a small plate on top of a ramekin and, holding plate and ramekin firmly in place, invert both and lift off ramekin. Repeat with remaining flans. Scatter each flan with a little chopped lobster and top with a slice of lobster. Serve warm or at room temperature, garnished with dill.

persimmon smoothie

Freeze a ripe Hachiya persimmon overnight. Halve and scoop out flesh. Blend with orange juice and plain yogurt to make a smoothie. Garnish with ground cinnamon or allspice.

yellow zucchini sauté

Cut yellow zucchini (courgettes) into thin lengthwise slices. Sauté in olive oil with minced garlic until lightly golden. Season with salt and pepper to taste. Garnish with minced fresh parsley and tarragon. Serve warm or cool.

kumquat salad

Toss thinly sliced kumquats with a mixture of minced fresh parsley and torn butter (Boston) lettuce leaves. Dress with a light vinaigrette made with extra-virgin olive oil and champagne vinegar.

tangy carrot salad

Peel and grate carrots. Make a vinaigrette with extra-virgin olive oil, red wine vinegar, Dijon mustard, and a little salt and pepper. Toss carrots in vinaigrette and garnish with minced fresh parsley or chopped green (spring) onions.

linguine with lemon & pecorino cheese

¾ lb (375 g) linguine

2 Tbsp extra-virgin olive oil

Grated zest of 1 lemon

1 tsp lemon juice

¼ cup (⅓ oz/10 g) minced fresh parsley

2–3 oz (60–90 g) pecorino cheese

In a large pot of salted boiling water, cook pasta until tender but firm, about 10 minutes. Drain.

Transfer pasta to a warmed serving bowl and add olive oil, ½ tsp salt, ½ tsp pepper, lemon zest and juice, and half of the parsley. Toss well to coat. Using a vegetable peeler, shave pecorino cheese into thin slices. Add all but 3 or 4 pieces to pasta and toss well. Garnish with remaining parsley and cheese. Serve hot.

To prepare: 10 minutes

To cook: 10 minutes

4 servings

yellow gazpacho

1½ lb (750 g) very ripe yellow tomatoes, peeled

1½ cucumbers

1 yellow bell pepper (capsicum)

2 tsp lemon juice

1 Tbsp extra-virgin olive oil

1 clove garlic, minced

Garnishes

1 cup (1½ oz/45 g) croutons

½ cucumber, peeled, seeded, and chopped

1 large, very ripe yellow tomato, peeled and chopped

⅓ cup (½ oz/15 g) chopped cilantro (fresh coriander)

Bring a large pot of water to a rolling boil. Score an X in the bottom of each tomato and plunge into the boiling water, 2 or 3 at a time, just until the skins start to wrinkle, about 30 seconds. Remove tomatoes with a slotted spoon and peel. Chop coarsely.

Peel, seed, and coarsely chop cucumbers, then seed bell pepper and chop coarsely.

Put vegetables in a food processor or blender with lemon juice and olive oil. Process until just blended and still slightly chunky. Pour into a nonreactive bowl and stir in garlic, ½ tsp salt, and 1 tsp pepper. Cover and refrigerate for at least 6 hours or up to overnight. Taste and adjust seasoning, adding up to ½ tsp salt if needed.

Serve the soup very cold, accompanied with garnishes.

To prepare: 20 minutes, plus 6–12 hours to chill

4 servings

orange pepper frittata with fresh thyme

6 eggs

2 Tbsp whole or low-fat milk

¼ cup (1 oz/30 g) grated Parmesan cheese

1 Tbsp butter

1 Tbsp olive oil

¼ onion, finely chopped

1 orange bell pepper (capsicum), seeded and finely chopped

1 Tbsp minced fresh thyme

1 Tbsp extra-virgin olive oil

In a large bowl, beat eggs, milk, and cheese together. Season with ¾ tsp salt and ½ tsp pepper. Set aside.

Melt butter with olive oil in a 10-inch (25-cm) frying pan over medium-high heat. Add onion and bell pepper. Sauté for 2 minutes, until onion is translucent, then reduce heat to medium and cook until pepper is soft, about 10 minutes. Pour egg mixture over vegetables. Reduce heat to low and cook until eggs are firm around edges, 3–4 minutes. Lift edges of eggs with a spatula and tilt pan to let uncooked eggs run under cooked eggs. Cook until eggs are almost set on top, about 5 minutes more.

Invert a plate on top of pan, hold plate and pan firmly together with pot holders, and invert. Slip frittata back into pan, cooked side up. Cook another minute or two. Invert a serving plate over pan and invert as before. Sprinkle with thyme. Serve hot or at room temperature. Cut into wedges, drizzle with extra-virgin olive oil, season to taste, and serve.

To prepare: 15 minutes

To cook: 30 minutes

4 servings

dried apricot canapés

16 thin baguette slices

6 oz (185 g) fontina cheese, thinly sliced

¾ cup (4 oz/125 g) dried apricots, chopped

⅓ cup (2 oz/60 g) toasted pine nuts (see page 121), chopped

Preheat oven to 400°F (200°C).

Top baguette slices with cheese and place on a baking sheet. Bake until cheese has melted, 7–10 minutes.

Remove baguette slices from oven and transfer to a serving platter. Top each with some apricots and pine nuts, pressing on toppings with your fingers to help secure them. Serve at once.

To prepare: 10 minutes

To cook: 10 minutes

4 or 5 servings (16 canapés)

grapefruit, chicken & pistachio salad

2 cups (16 fl oz/500 ml) dry white wine

2 Tbsp white wine vinegar

1 tsp whole peppercorns

2 skinless, boneless chicken breast halves

2 grapefruits, peeled, segmented (see page 103), and seeded

½ cup (2 oz/60 g) unsalted pistachios, toasted (see page 121)

¼ cup (2 fl oz/60 ml) mayonnaise

1 tsp Dijon mustard

2 Tbsp minced cilantro (fresh coriander)

Juice of 1 lime

4 leaves romaine (cos) lettuce

Paprika for sprinkling

Combine wine, 2 cups (16 fl oz/500 ml) water, vinegar, 1 tsp salt, and peppercorns in a shallow pan. Bring to a boil over medium-high heat. Reduce heat to low and simmer for 5 minutes. Add chicken, cover, and poach until just opaque, 6–8 minutes. Remove chicken from liquid and let cool for 5 minutes, then cut into cubes.

Cut grapefruit segments in half crosswise. Put in a bowl with chicken and half of the pistachios. Add mayonnaise, mustard, cilantro, lime juice, ½ tsp salt, and ¼ tsp pepper and mix well.

Divide lettuce leaves among 4 salad plates. Fill each leaf with chicken salad, sprinkle with paprika, and garnish with remaining pistachios. Serve at once.

To prepare: 20 minutes

To cook: 8 minutes

4 servings

yellow beet & yellow pear tomato salad

4 yellow beets, greens trimmed to 2 inches (5 cm)

2 tsp extra-virgin olive oil, plus ¼ cup (2 fl oz/60 ml)

20 fresh purple or green basil leaves

½ lb (250 g) fresh mozzarella, cut into slices ¼ inch (6 mm) thick

2 cups (12 oz/375 g) yellow pear tomatoes, halved lengthwise

1 Tbsp sherry vinegar

Preheat oven to 350°F (180°C).

Rub beets with 2 tsp olive oil and put in a baking dish. Bake until fork-tender, about 1 hour. Remove from oven and let cool. Trim, peel, and cut into slices ¼ inch (6 mm) thick. Tear large basil leaves into pieces, leaving small ones whole.

Overlap beets and cheese on a serving platter in single layer. Sprinkle tomatoes over, then sprinkle with ½ tsp salt and ½ tsp pepper. Tuck basil leaves between layers, then drizzle vinegar and ¼ cup olive oil over all and serve.

To prepare: 20 minutes

To cook: 1 hour

6 servings

rhubarb cranberries red onions

RED FRUITS AND VEGETABLES PROVIDE ANTIOXIDANTS

ruby grapefruit radishes beets

FOR PROTECTION AND HEALING • PROMOTE HEART

cherries watermelon red plums

HEALTH • PROMOTE URINARY TRACT HEALTH • HELP

tomatoes red pears raspberries

REDUCE THE RISK OF CERTAIN CANCERS • IMPROVE

pomegranates red bell peppers

MEMORY FUNCTION • RED FRUITS AND VEGETABLES

radicchio strawberries quinces

OFFER ANTIOXIDANTS FOR PROTECTION AND HEALING

Red

Brilliant red fruits and vegetables add excitement to any plate but are an especially eye-catching way to start a meal. The intense color of this group is matched by the intense tastes of favorite fruits such as cherries and strawberries and vegetables that run the gamut from bitter radishes to sugar-sweet beets. This chapter offers an array of interesting ways to add more red to your table.

Red fruits and vegetables are among the produce highest in antioxidants, with cranberries, strawberries, and raspberries leading the charge, and cherries and red grapes following not far behind. Red beets and red bell peppers are not only delicious additions to soups and salads, but they are also rich in vitamins and minerals.

When you start a meal with Red Onion Marmalade & Pork Canapés (page 94), Roasted Tomato Soup with Basil (page 100), or Ruby Grapefruit and Pomegranate Salad (page 103), you will be treating your senses as well as helping yourself (and your family or guests) stay healthy, filling your meals with vitamin C and other nutrients.

This chapter includes a red bouquet of refreshing and interesting openers, such as Smoked Gouda Toasts with Rhubarb Chutney (page 103), the perfect addition to a party buffet, and Red Apple, Walnut, and Stilton Salad (page 93), a light start to any winter meal. It's easy to spark your palate and your day with a flash of healthy red.

SPRING	SUMMER	AUTUMN	WINTER
beets	cherries	red apples	red apples
pink or red grapefruit	red bell peppers	beets	beets
red onions	red chiles	red bell peppers	cranberries
blood oranges	red onions	red chiles	pink or red grapefruit
red potatoes	red plums	cranberries	red grapes
radicchio	radishes	red grapes	blood oranges
radishes	raspberries	red pears	pomegranates
rhubarb	rhubarb	red plums	red potatoes
strawberries	strawberries	pomegranates	quinces
	tomatoes	red potatoes	radicchio
	watermelon	quinces	radishes
		raspberries	

smoked trout salad with blood orange dressing

¾ cup (6 fl oz/180 ml) blood orange juice (from about 3 oranges), plus 1 blood orange, segmented (see page 103)

¼ cup (2 fl oz/60 ml) lemon juice

1 Tbsp extra-virgin olive oil

1 tsp minced shallot

2 bunches watercress, stemmed, about 4 cups (4 oz/125 g)

⅓ lb (5 oz/155 g) smoked trout

Combine orange and lemon juice in a saucepan and bring to a boil over medium heat. Cook to reduce to about ½ cup (4 fl oz/125 ml). Remove from heat and let cool. Stir in olive oil and shallot to make a dressing. Season to taste with salt and pepper.

Put watercress in a bowl and pour over all but 2 Tbsp of dressing. Toss to coat evenly. Divide watercress evenly among individual bowls or plates. Break trout into pieces and arrange on top of greens. Drizzle each serving with a little dressing. Garnish each salad with an orange segment or two and serve at once.

Note: If blood oranges are not available, substitute navel oranges and use raspberry vinegar instead of lemon juice.

To prepare: 10 minutes

To cook: 5 minutes

4 servings

red apple, walnut & stilton salad

4 unpeeled red apples

1 cup (1 oz/30 g) mixed salad greens

2 Tbsp mayonnaise

1 Tbsp whole or low-fat milk

1 tsp lemon juice

½ tsp sugar

2 oz (60 g) Stilton cheese, sliced, at room temperature

½ cup (2 oz/60 g) walnut pieces, toasted (see page 121)

Cut apples in half and core with a small, sharp knife. Cut into thin slices. Divide greens among 4 salad plates and arrange apple slices on top.

In a small bowl, mix together mayonnaise, milk, lemon juice, sugar, and ¼ tsp salt to make a dressing. Drizzle over greens and apples. Top with Stilton cheese slices, sprinkle with walnuts, and serve.

To prepare: 15 minutes

4 servings

red onion marmalade & pork canapés

2 Tbsp butter

3 Tbsp olive oil

2 red onions, finely chopped

¼ cup (2 fl oz/60 ml) Cognac or brandy

¼ cup (2 fl oz/60 ml) red wine vinegar

¼ cup (2 oz/60 g) packed light brown sugar

3 tsp minced fresh thyme

1 pork tenderloin, about ¾ lb (375 g)

15 baguette slices, ¼ inch (6 mm) thick

Melt butter with 2 Tbsp of olive oil in a saucepan over medium-high heat. Add onions and sauté until nearly soft, about 2 minutes. Add Cognac, vinegar, sugar, and 1 tsp thyme, stirring until sugar dissolves, about 2 minutes. Reduce heat to low, cover, and simmer until mixture is thick and almost dry, about 30 minutes. If liquid evaporates before onions are cooked, add a little water. Remove from heat and set aside.

Preheat oven to 450°F (230°C).

Season pork with 1 tsp salt, 1 tsp pepper, and remaining thyme. Heat remaining olive oil over medium-high heat in an ovenproof frying pan. Brown pork on all sides, 4–5 minutes. Put frying pan in oven and roast pork until an instant-read thermometer registers 150°F (65°C) when inserted into center of meat, 12–15 minutes. Remove to a cutting board, loosely tent with foil, and let rest for 5 minutes.

Thinly slice pork. Top each slice of bread with a little onion marmalade and place a slice of pork on it. Serve.

To prepare: 15 minutes

To cook: 1 hour

4–6 servings
(12–15 canapés)

grapes with roquefort & almond coating

½ cup (2 oz/60 g) raw or blanched almonds, toasted (see page 121)

4 oz (125 g) Roquefort cheese at room temperature

2–3 Tbsp whole or low-fat milk

20 seedless red grapes

Parsley sprigs for garnish (optional)

Pulse almonds to a medium-fine texture in a blender or small food processor. Spread on a plate and set aside.

Put cheese in a bowl and mash it with a fork. Add milk and mix to make a spreadable paste. Using your fingers, pat a coating of cheese around each grape and then roll in almonds to cover. Arrange grapes on a platter, garnish with parsley, and serve.

Note: If you like, serve coated grapes interspersed with uncoated ones.

To prepare: 20 minutes

4 servings

red beet pancakes with yogurt & dill

4 red beets

2 eggs, beaten

½ cup (2½ oz/75 g) all-purpose (plain) flour

1–2 Tbsp canola oil

¾ cup (6 oz/185 g) plain whole or low-fat yogurt

½ cup (½ oz/15 g) fresh dill sprigs for garnish

Peel beets using a small, sharp knife or vegetable peeler, then shred using a box grater. Combine shredded beets, eggs, flour, ½ tsp salt, and ½ tsp pepper in a bowl and mix well to make a batter.

Heat 2 tsp of oil in a nonstick frying pan over medium-high heat and add heaping tablespoons batter, 3 inches (7.5 cm) apart. Flatten with a metal spatula and cook until lightly browned, 2–3 minutes per side. Remove to a plate lined with paper towels and keep warm in a low (150°F/65°C) oven. Repeat to cook remaining batter. Serve at once, topped with yogurt and fresh dill.

To prepare: 15 minutes

To cook: 20 minutes

5 or 6 servings
(16–20 pancakes)

strawberry & cherry salad

Toss pitted and halved fresh cherries and hulled and halved fresh strawberries with baby spinach and drizzle with an orange juice vinaigrette. Garnish with chopped toasted and skinned hazelnuts (filberts) or toasted walnuts, if desired.

roasted pomegranate

Roast a pomegranate in a preheated 400°F (200°C) oven until cooked through, 20–25 minutes. Split in half and drizzle with lemon juice, extra-virgin olive oil, and honey. Sprinkle with salt and minced fresh mint.

grilled radicchio with anchovy sauce

Cut radicchio into quarters. Drizzle with olive oil and sprinkle with minced fresh thyme, salt, and pepper. Grill or broil (grill) until browned on each side. Sauté anchovy fillets with olive oil, mashing to make a sauce. Spoon over radicchio.

pomegranate spritzer

Mix pomegranate juice and seeds with crushed ice and a lightly chilled rosé wine to make a refreshing spritzer. Or, add a little juice to champagne to make a pomegranate kir royal. Enjoy as an *aperitivo* or midafternoon pick-me-up.

roasted tomato soup with basil

4 lb (2 kg) very ripe red tomatoes

4 oz (125 g) oil-cured black olives, pitted and chopped

1 tsp minced fresh thyme

2 cloves garlic, minced

1 cup (1 oz/30 g) fresh basil leaves, plus chopped basil for garnish

2 shallots, minced

1 tsp fennel seeds

One 2-inch (5-cm) strip orange zest

1 Tbsp orange juice

¼ cup (2 fl oz/60 ml) extra-virgin olive oil

Preheat oven to 400°F (200°C).

Cut tomatoes in half crosswise and place in a roasting pan, cut side down. Sprinkle tomatoes with olives, thyme, garlic, 1 cup basil, shallots, fennel seeds, orange zest, orange juice, ½ tsp salt, and ½ tsp pepper. Pour olive oil over and roast until tomatoes have released their juices and collapsed, 30–40 minutes.

Remove from oven and purée in a blender or food processer. Strain mixture through a fine-mesh sieve, pressing on solids with back of a large spoon, into a clean saucepan. Bring to a simmer over medium-low heat. Add salt and pepper to taste and cook, stirring, to meld flavors, about 3 minutes.

To serve, ladle hot soup into warmed bowls and garnish each with chopped basil.

To prepare: 15 minutes

To cook: 45 minutes

4 servings

watermelon, raspberry & mint salad

4 cups (about 2 lb/1 kg) seeded and cubed watermelon

⅓ cup (½ oz/15 g) minced fresh mint, plus 4 sprigs for garnish

3 cups (12 oz/375 g) fresh raspberries

1 Tbsp honey

2 tsp lime juice

Divide watermelon cubes among 4 salad bowls. Sprinkle with most of the minced mint. Top with equal amounts of raspberries and sprinkle with remaining minced mint.

In a small bowl, mix honey and lime juice together with a fork or small whisk and drizzle a little over each salad. Garnish with a sprig of mint.

To prepare: 15 minutes

4 servings

ruby grapefruit & pomegranate salad

3 ruby grapefruits

1 Tbsp champagne vinegar

2 Tbsp extra-virgin olive oil

1 tsp sugar

1 Tbsp minced fresh chervil, tarragon, or parsley

2 cups (2 oz/60 g) butter (Boston) lettuce leaves

Seeds from 1 small pomegranate, about 1 cup (4 oz/125 g)

To segment grapefruit, slice off top and bottom to expose flesh. Stand on a flat end. Using a sharp knife to follow curve of sides, cut off peel down to flesh. Holding fruit over a bowl, cut segments free of membrane on each side. Squeeze membranes over bowl to release juice.

Combine vinegar, olive oil, sugar, chervil, and ¼ tsp salt in a salad bowl. Tear lettuce leaves and add to bowl. Add grapefruit segments and juice and pomegranate seeds and toss well to coat evenly. Serve at once.

To prepare: 10 minutes

4 servings

smoked gouda toasts with rhubarb chutney

1 cup (7 oz/220 g) packed brown sugar

½ cup (4 fl oz/125 ml) cider vinegar

1 Tbsp grated lemon zest

3 or 4 rhubarb stalks, cut into 1-inch (2.5-cm) pieces

1 cinnamon stick

¼ cup (1½ oz/45 g) minced fresh ginger

½ cup (3 oz/90 g) golden raisins (sultanas)

¼ cup (1 oz/30 g) chopped walnuts

4 slices brioche or other fine bread

2–3 oz (60–90 g) smoked Gouda cheese, thinly sliced

Combine sugar, vinegar, and lemon zest in a nonreactive saucepan and cook over low heat, stirring, until sugar dissolves, about 5 minutes. Add rhubarb, cinnamon stick, and ginger. Raise heat to medium and cook, stirring often, until rhubarb is soft, about 15 minutes. Remove cinnamon stick and discard. Add raisins, walnuts, and ⅛ tsp salt. Cook for about 3 minutes. Remove from heat and let cool.

Toast brioche slices in a toaster. Let cool slightly and cut into triangles. Place a slice or two of smoked Gouda on each triangle and top with a little chutney.

Note: You can store leftover chutney in an airtight jar in refrigerator for up to 2 weeks.

To prepare: 15 minutes

To cook: 25 minutes

4 servings

roasted red potato canapés with salmon roe

6 small red potatoes, each about 1½ inches (4 cm) in diameter, scrubbed

1 Tbsp extra-virgin olive oil

2 Tbsp crème fraîche

4 tsp salmon roe

2 Tbsp minced fresh chives

Preheat oven to 350°F (180°C).

Rub potatoes with olive oil and put in a baking dish. Roast until fork-tender, 45–60 minutes. Remove from oven, let cool, and cut in half. Using a teaspoon or melon baller, scoop out centers, leaving a generous ¼-inch (6-mm) rim. Put scooped-out potato flesh in a bowl and add ¼ tsp salt, ½ tsp pepper, and 1 Tbsp crème fraîche. Mash the mixture together with a fork.

Fill each scooped-out potato half with potato mixture. Sprinkle with salt, dollop with a little of the remaining crème fraîche, and sprinkle with salmon roe, chives, and freshly ground pepper. Serve warm.

To prepare: 25 minutes

To cook: 1 hour

4 servings

prosciutto-wrapped radicchio wedges

6 tsp extra-virgin olive oil

1 medium to large head radicchio

6 thin slices prosciutto

¼ cup (1 oz/30 g) grated Parmesan cheese

Preheat oven to 350°F (180°C).

Drizzle 2 tsp olive oil into a baking dish just large enough to hold wrapped radicchio slices snugly.

Cut radicchio lengthwise into 6 slices. Put radicchio slices in prepared baking dish and drizzle with 3 tsp olive oil, turning them once or twice to coat them well. Sprinkle with ½ tsp pepper. Remove slices and fold a slice of prosciutto around each one. Lay wrapped pieces back in baking dish, drizzle with remaining olive oil, and sprinkle with cheese. Place in oven and bake until cheese is browned and radicchio is fork-tender, 15–20 minutes. Serve at once.

To prepare: 10 minutes

To cook: 20 minutes

6 servings

soybeans brown rice garbanzos

WHOLE GRAINS, LEGUMES, SEEDS, AND NUTS PROMOTE

pecans chestnuts bulgur wheat

ARTERY AND HEART HEALTH • HELP REDUCE THE RISK

flaxseed sesame seeds polenta

OF DIABETES • REDUCE HIGH BLOOD PRESSURE • OFFER

pumpkin seeds cashews quinoa

ANTIOXIDANTS FOR PROTECTION AND HEALING • HELP

kasha macadamia nuts walnuts

REDUCE THE RISK OF STROKE • MAY REDUCE THE RISK

hazelnuts oats couscous millet

OF CANCERS OF THE BREAST, PROSTATE, AND COLON

Brown

This chapter adds another color band to the healthy eating rainbow to accommodate grains, legumes, seeds, and nuts. Their colors may range from the red of kidney beans to the yellow of split peas, but you can think of them as brown foods as a convenient way to group them to serve and to remember the importance of bringing unrefined, natural foods into your daily diet.

Most unrefined grains are brown, because their bran has not been removed. It is this coating, along with the oil- and nutrient-rich germ, that makes whole grains so important in the diet. Whole grains from barley to polenta are suddenly in culinary vogue, and they deserve the spotlight because of the satisfying flavors and textures they offer.

Our modern diet has come to exclude whole grains, but the starters in this chapter will help you to bring them back to your table, with simple and tempting dishes like Bulgur Salad with Lemon, Peas, and Mint (page 118) and Millet Salad with Mango and Cilantro (page 118). Legumes, which include peas, beans, and peanuts, are high in both protein and fiber and are represented here in dishes such as Lentil Soup (page 122) and Split Pea Soup with Tarragon Cream (page 112).

Nuts and seeds are used in this chapter not just because they are also high in protein and important minerals but because they add delightful taste and crunch to salads, soups, and other delicious first courses.

GRAINS	LEGUMES	SEEDS	NUTS
barley	black beans	flaxseed	almonds
bulgur wheat	cannellini beans	pumpkin seeds	Brazil nuts
couscous (wheat pasta)	chickpeas	sesame seeds	cashews
kasha (buckwheat groats)	kidney beans	sunflower seeds	chestnuts
millet	lima beans		hazelnuts
oats	soybeans		macadamia nuts
polenta (ground corn)	black-eyed peas		pecans
quinoa	split peas		pine nuts
brown rice	lentils		pistachio nuts
whole wheat	peanuts		walnuts

pork satay with peanut sauce

1 lb (500 g) boneless pork loin

½ cup (4 fl oz/125 ml) coconut milk or condensed milk

3 Tbsp minced shallots

1 tsp ground coriander

1 tsp ground cumin

1 tsp ground turmeric

2 Tbsp fish sauce

1 tsp light soy sauce

2 Tbsp packed brown sugar

Asian Peanut Sauce

½ cup (5 oz/155 g) creamy peanut butter

⅓ cup (3 fl oz/80 ml) chicken broth

2 Tbsp orange juice

1 Tbsp soy sauce

½ Tbsp lemon juice

½ tsp Asian sesame oil

1 or 2 cloves garlic, chopped

½ Tbsp minced fresh ginger

½ small habanero or jalapeño chile, seeded and chopped

1½ Tbsp chopped fresh mint

Cut pork crosswise into strips 2 inches (5 cm) long and ½ inch (12 mm) wide. Combine coconut milk, shallots, coriander, cumin, turmeric, fish sauce, soy sauce, and sugar in a blender and purée to make a marinade.

Put meat in a shallow baking dish and pour marinade over. Stir to coat meat well. Let stand at room temperature for up to 1 hour, or cover and refrigerate up to overnight.

If refrigerated, remove meat from refrigerator 30 minutes before cooking. Soak 12–14 long wooden skewers in water for 30 minutes.

For Peanut Sauce: In a food processor, combine peanut butter, broth, orange juice, soy sauce, lemon juice, sesame oil, garlic, ginger, and chile. Process, stopping several times to scrape down sides of work bowl, until smooth. Let stand at room temperature for 1 hour, or cover and refrigerate for up to 24 hours to develop flavors. If refrigerated, return to room temperature. Stir in chopped mint just before serving.

Build a hot wood or charcoal fire in a grill, or preheat a gas grill to 400°F (200°C). Thread 3 pieces of meat on each skewer. Grill until browned, 1–2 minutes per side. Serve hot, accompanied with peanut sauce.

To prepare: 1 hour 15 minutes

To cook: 4 minutes

4 servings

black bean & fresh corn tostadas

1 Tbsp olive oil

Kernels cut from 1 ear yellow corn

2 cups (14 oz/440 g) drained cooked black beans, or one 14-oz (440-g) can black beans, drained

½ tsp ground cumin

4 corn tortillas, warmed

Plain whole or low-fat yogurt, avocado slices, and minced fresh cilantro (fresh coriander) for garnish

Heat olive oil in a saucepan over medium heat and add corn kernels, ½ tsp salt, and ½ tsp pepper. Cook, stirring, until corn is just heated through and slightly tender, about 3 minutes.

Combine beans and corn in a bowl and season with salt and pepper to taste and cumin. Top each tortilla with bean mixture, then add a spoonful of yogurt, a slice or two of avocado, and a sprinkling of minced cilantro. Serve at once.

To prepare: 15 minutes

To cook: 4 minutes

4 servings

split pea soup with tarragon cream

¼ cup (2 oz/60 g) low-fat sour cream

2 Tbsp minced fresh tarragon

1 Tbsp olive oil

2 Tbsp finely chopped onion

1½ cups (10½ oz/330 g) green split peas, rinsed and picked over

Put sour cream in a bowl and stir in tarragon. Set aside.

Heat olive oil in a saucepan over medium heat. Add onion and sauté until translucent, about 2 minutes. Add peas and stir several times. Add 5 cups (40 fl oz/1.25 l) water and 1 tsp salt and raise heat to high. Bring to a boil, reduce heat to low, and cover. Simmer until peas are tender, 45–50 minutes. Purée soup in a blender. Return to same pan and bring to a simmer. Add salt and pepper to taste.

Ladle hot soup into warmed bowls and add a dollop of tarragon cream to each. Serve at once.

To prepare: 10 minutes

To cook: 60 minutes

4 servings

quinoa & grilled summer vegetables

1 cup (6 oz/185 g) quinoa

1 zucchini (courgette), thinly sliced lengthwise

2 Japanese eggplants (aubergines), thinly sliced lengthwise

8 oz (250 g) green beans, trimmed

1 red bell pepper (capsicum), seeded and cut into strips ½ inch (12 mm) wide

½ cup (4 oz/125 g) oil-cured black olives, pitted

¼ cup (2 fl oz/60 ml) extra-virgin olive oil, plus more for drizzling (optional)

2 cloves garlic, crushed

3 or 4 thyme sprigs

2 or 3 rosemary sprigs

1 bay leaf

2 Tbsp fresh basil chiffonade

Bring 2 cups (16 fl oz/500 ml) water to a boil in a saucepan and add quinoa and ½ tsp salt. Return to a boil, then reduce heat to low, cover, and simmer until quinoa is tender and the water is absorbed, about 20 minutes.

Meanwhile, build a hot charcoal or wood fire in a grill, or preheat a gas grill to 400°F (200°C).

Combine zucchini, eggplants, green beans, bell pepper, and olives in a bowl. Add olive oil, garlic, thyme, rosemary, bay leaf, 1 tsp salt, and ½ tsp pepper. Toss to blend. Let stand for 30 minutes, tossing frequently. Place vegetables in a single layer in an oiled grill basket and grill until lightly browned, about 5 minutes per side.

Season quinoa with salt and pepper, and drizzle with olive oil if desired. Mound quinoa on a serving platter or individual plates. Top with grilled vegetables and sprinkle with basil. Serve warm.

To prepare: 20 minutes

To cook: 25 minutes, plus 30 minutes to stand

4 servings

mixed spiced nuts & peanuts

Preheat oven to 300°F (150°C). Toss almonds, walnuts, and peanuts with olive oil, paprika, ground cumin, sugar, and coarse salt. Spread nuts on a baking sheet and bake, shaking occasionally, for 15 minutes. Let cool and serve.

cashews in fruit salads

Chopped cashews add protein and a crunchy texture to fruit salads. Try adding them to sliced bananas, sliced oranges, and chopped cilantro (fresh coriander). Dress with a few drops of sesame oil and rice vinegar.

crisp polenta with blue cheese

Make polenta cut-outs (see page 52) in the shape of diamonds. Heat olive oil in a large pan and fry the polenta, turning once, until golden. Drain and top with crumbled blue cheese and a scattering of baby arugula (rocket) leaves.

scrambled eggs with flaxseed & chives

Whisk eggs in a bowl just until blended. Cook in a double boiler over simmering water, stirring, just until soft curds form. Add salt and pepper to taste, minced fresh chives, and some flaxseed. Serve on toasted walnut bread.

bulgur salad with lemon, peas & mint

1 cup (6 oz/185 g) bulgur wheat

1 Tbsp plus 2 tsp extra-virgin olive oil

2/3 lb (10 oz/315 g) sugar snap peas, sliced on diagonal (about 2 cups)

1/3 cup (1/2 oz/15 g) minced fresh mint, plus sprigs for garnish

1 Tbsp lemon juice

1 Tbsp capers, chopped

2 oil-packed sun-dried tomatoes, chopped

In a saucepan, bring 2 cups (16 fl oz/500 ml) water to a boil. Add bulgur and 1/2 tsp salt. Return to a boil, then reduce heat to low. Cover and cook until bulgur is tender and water is absorbed, about 20 minutes.

Combine bulgur and 2 tsp olive oil in a bowl, turning gently to coat and fluff grains. Let cool to room temperature. Add peas, minced mint, lemon juice, capers, sun-dried tomatoes, 1/2 tsp salt, 1/2 tsp pepper, and remaining 1 Tbsp oil. Stir well to blend.

Put in a serving bowl and garnish with mint sprigs. Serve at room temperature.

To prepare: 15 minutes

To cook: 25 minutes

4 servings

millet salad with mango & cilantro

1 Tbsp olive oil (optional)

1 cup (6 oz/185 g) millet

1 large mango, peeled, pitted, and cut into 1/2-inch (12-mm) dice

1/3 cup (1/2 oz/15 g) minced cilantro (fresh coriander), plus sprigs for garnish

1 Tbsp lime juice

If desired, heat olive oil in frying pan over medium heat and sauté millet briefly.

Bring 2 cups (16 fl oz/500 ml) water to a boil in a saucepan over medium-high heat. Add millet and 1/2 tsp salt. Return to a boil, reduce heat to low, cover, and simmer until millet is tender and water is absorbed, about 20 minutes. Remove millet to a large platter and spread in a thin layer to cool.

Combine mango, minced cilantro, and lime juice in a bowl. Fluff millet with a fork, then add it to bowl and toss to mix.

Divide the salad among 4 plates and garnish with a sprig of cilantro. Serve at room temperature.

To prepare: 15 minutes

To cook: 25 minutes

4 servings

white bean & sage crostini

⅓ cup (3 fl oz/80 ml) olive oil

1 clove garlic, minced

One 15-oz (470-g) can cannellini or other white beans, drained (liquid reserved)

2 Tbsp minced fresh sage

12 slices baguette

¼ cup (1 oz/30 g) roasted red pepper strips or oil-packed sun-dried tomatoes

Heat olive oil in a frying pan over medium-high heat. Add garlic and sauté until soft, about 1 minute. Add beans, sage, 1 tsp salt, and ½ tsp pepper and cook, stirring often, until beans are heated through, about 2 minutes. Remove to a food processor and coarsely process, adding a little reserved bean liquid if needed to make a spreadable paste.

Toast baguette slices in a toaster or on a baking sheet in a preheated 350°F (180°C) oven until golden, about 5 minutes per side. Spread each toast with some of the beans and top with a strip of roasted red pepper or sun-dried tomato.

To prepare: 15 minutes

To cook: 12 minutes

4 servings

orzo salad with cucumber

¼ cup (1 oz/30 g) chopped raw or blanched almonds

1 cup (7 oz/220 g) orzo pasta

2 Tbsp extra-virgin olive oil

1 cucumber, peeled and halved lengthwise

3 Tbsp minced fresh mint

3 Tbsp minced fresh basil

2 Tbsp minced fresh tarragon

⅓ cup (1½ oz/45 g) finely chopped red onion

4 oil-packed sun-dried tomatoes, chopped

2 tsp lemon juice

Preheat oven to 300°F (150°C).

Spread almonds on a baking pan and bake until lightly golden, about 7 minutes. Remove from oven and set aside.

In a large pot of salted boiling water, cook orzo until firm but tender, about 12 minutes. Drain. Put in a bowl, add 1 Tbsp olive oil, and toss to coat completely.

With a spoon, seed cucumber. Cut cucumber halves crosswise into half-moons ¼ inch (6 mm) wide. Add to orzo along with mint, basil, tarragon, onion, sun-dried tomatoes, lemon juice, ½ tsp salt, ½ tsp pepper, and remaining oil. Toss to mix well.

Serve warm or at room temperature, sprinkled with toasted almonds.

To prepare: 15 minutes

To cook: 20 minutes

4 servings

hummus with pita points

3 pita bread rounds

One 15-oz (470-g) can chickpeas
(garbanzo beans)

1 Tbsp tahini

¼ cup (2 fl oz/60 ml) lemon juice

2 cloves garlic, minced

¼ cup (2 fl oz/60 ml) extra-virgin
olive oil, plus 1 Tbsp

½ tsp ground cumin

⅛ tsp cayenne pepper

3 Tbsp minced fresh parsley

1 tsp paprika

Preheat oven to 400°F (200°C).

Cut each pita round into 8 triangles and place on a baking sheet. Bake until slightly crisp, 10–15 minutes. Set aside.

Drain chickpeas, reserving liquid. In a food processor, purée chickpeas with tahini, lemon juice, garlic, ¼ cup olive oil, cumin, ½ tsp salt, and cayenne. If mixture is too thick, add a little reserved bean liquid.

Spoon into a bowl and garnish with parsley, paprika, and 1 Tbsp olive oil. Serve with pita bread toasts.

To prepare: 15 minutes

To cook: 15 minutes

4 servings

lentil soup

2 thick slices bacon, cut into
¼-inch (6-mm) pieces

1 clove garlic, minced

½ small onion, finely chopped

2 carrots, unpeeled and finely
chopped

1 stalk celery, finely chopped

1½ cups (10½ oz/330 g) small green
(French) lentils

2 tsp fresh thyme leaves

1 bay leaf

2 oil-packed sun-dried tomatoes,
chopped, for garnish

In a saucepan over medium heat, cook bacon, stirring occasionally, until lightly golden, about 5 minutes. Add garlic, onion, carrots, and celery and sauté until the onion is translucent and the vegetables are soft, about 3 minutes. Add lentils and stir well. Add 4–4½ cups (32–36 fl oz/1–1.1 l) water, thyme, 1 tsp salt, ½ tsp pepper, and bay leaf. Reduce heat to low and simmer, adding more water if needed, until lentils are tender but firm, 30–40 minutes.

Ladle into warmed bowls, garnish with chopped sun-dried tomatoes, and serve at once.

To prepare: 15 minutes

To cook: 40 minutes

4 servings

buckwheat pancakes with tomato-corn salsa

Salsa

Kernels from 2 ears white corn

1 serrano chile, seeded and minced

1 lb (500 g) ripe tomatoes, chopped

2 Tbsp finely chopped onion

3 Tbsp minced fresh cilantro (fresh coriander)

4 tsp lime juice

Pancakes

½ cup (2½ oz/75 g) buckwheat flour

¼ cup (1½ oz/45 g) all-purpose (plain) flour

¾ tsp baking powder

1 Tbsp minced fresh parsley

¾ cup (6 fl oz/180 ml) whole or low-fat milk

3 Tbsp canola oil

1 egg

For Salsa: Combine corn kernels, chile, tomatoes, onion, cilantro, lime juice, ½ tsp salt, and ½ tsp pepper in a bowl and toss to mix well. Set salsa aside.

For Pancakes: In a large bowl, combine flours, baking powder, ¼ tsp salt, and parsley. Stir to blend. In another bowl, whisk together milk, 2 Tbsp oil, and egg until blended. Gradually stir wet ingredients into dry ingredients just until blended; do not overmix.

Heat remaining 1 Tbsp oil in a frying pan over medium-high heat. Ladle in 2-Tbsp portions of batter per pancake, 2 inches (5 cm) apart. When surface of cakes bubble and underside is lightly browned, turn and cook on other side until lightly browned, about 2 minutes per side. Transfer to a platter and keep warm in a low oven. Repeat to cook remaining batter.

Serve hot or warm, with salsa on top.

To prepare: 20 minutes

To cook: 15 minutes

12 small pancakes, 4 servings

Nutrients at work

Humans need more than forty nutrients to support life. Many foods are good sources of many different nutrients, but no single food provides everything. Eating a variety of foods, preferably in their whole form, is the best way to get all the nutrients your body needs. Some nutrients require others for optimal absorption, but excessive amounts may result in heath problems.

Until recently, nutrition experts recommended the distribution of carbohydrates, protein, and fat in a well-balanced diet to be 55 percent of calories from carbohydrates, 15 percent of calories from protein, and 30 percent of calories from fat. As we have learned more about individual health needs and differences in metabolism, we have become more flexible in determining what constitutes a healthy diet. The table below shows macro-nutrient ranges recommended in September 2002 by the Institute of Medicine, part of the U.S. National Academies. These ranges are more likely to accommodate everyone's health needs. To help you evaluate and balance your diet as you prepare the recipes in this book, turn to pages 130–33 for nutritional analyses of each recipe.

Nutrition experts have also determined guidelines for vitamins and minerals. For more information, see pages 128–29.

CARBOHYDRATES, PROTEIN, AND FATS

NUTRIENTS AND FOOD SOURCES	FUNCTIONS	RECOMMENDED % OF DAILY CALORIES AND GUIDANCE
Carbohydrates COMPLEX CARBOHYDRATES • Grains, breads, cereals, pastas • Dried beans and peas, lentils • Starchy vegetables (potatoes, corn, green peas)	• Main source of energy for the body • Particularly important for the brain and nervous system • Fiber aids normal digestion	45–65% • Favor complex carbohydrates, especially legumes, vegetables, and whole grains (brown rice; whole-grain bread, pasta, and cereal). • Many foods high in complex carbohydrates are also good fiber sources. Among the best are bran cereals, canned and dried beans, dried fruit, and rolled oats. Recommended daily intake of fiber for adults under age 50 is 25 g for women and 38 g for men. For women over age 50, intake is 21 g; for men, 30 g.
SIMPLE CARBOHYDRATES • Naturally occurring sugars in fruits, vegetables, and milk • Added refined sugars in soft drinks, candy, baked goods, jams and jellies, etc.	• Provide energy	• Fruit and vegetables have naturally occurring sugars but also have vitamins, minerals, and phytochemicals. Refined sugar, on the other hand, has little to offer in the way of nutrition, so limit your intake to get the most from your daily calories.

Source: Institute of Medicine. Dietary Reference Intakes for Energy, Carbohydrates, Fiber, Fat, Protein and Amino Acids (Macronutrients).

CARBOHYDRATES, PROTEIN, AND FATS

NUTRIENTS AND FOOD SOURCES	FUNCTIONS	RECOMMENDED % OF DAILY CALORIES AND GUIDANCE
Protein • Foods from animal sources • Dried beans and peas, nuts • Grain products	• Builds and repairs cells • Regulates body processes by providing components for enzymes, hormones, fluid balance, nerve transmission	**10–35%** • Choose lean sources such as dried beans, fish, poultry, lean cuts of meat, soy, and low-fat dairy products most of the time. • Egg yolks are rich in many nutrients but also high in cholesterol; limit to 5 per week.
Fats All fats are mixtures of saturated and unsaturated (polyunsaturated and mono-unsaturated) types. Polyunsaturated and especially monounsaturated types are considered more desirable because they promote cardiovascular health.	• Supplies essential fatty acids needed for various body processes and to build cell membranes, particularly of the brain and nervous system • Transports certain vitamins	**20–35%** • Experts disagree about the ideal amount of total fat in the diet. Some say more is fine if it is heart-healthy fat; others recommend limiting total fat. Virtually all experts agree that saturated fat, trans fats, and cholesterol, all of which can raise "bad" (LDL) cholesterol, should be limited.
PRIMARILY SATURATED • Foods from animal sources (meat fat, butter, cheese, cream) • Coconut, palm, palm kernel oils	• Raises blood levels of "bad" (LDL) cholesterol	• Limit saturated fat.
PRIMARILY POLYUNSATURATED (PUFA) • Omega-3 fatty acids: herring, salmon, mackerel, lake trout, sardines, sword fish, nuts, flaxseed, canola oil, soy bean oil, tofu • Omega-6: vegetable oils such as corn, soybean, and safflower (abundant in the American diet)	• Reduces inflammation; influences blood clotting and blood vessel activity to improve blood flow	• Eat fish at least twice a week. • Substitute PUFA for saturated fat or trans fat when possible.
PRIMARILY MONOUNSATURATED (MUFA) Olive oil, canola oil, sesame oil, avocados, almonds, chicken fat	• Raises blood levels of "good" (HDL) cholesterol	• Substitute MUFA for saturated fat or trans fat when possible.
DIETARY CHOLESTEROL Foods from animal sources (egg yolks, organ meats, cheese, fish roe, meat)	• A structural component of cell membranes and some hormones	• The body makes cholesterol, and some foods contain dietary cholesterol. U.S. food labels list cholesterol values.
Trans fat Processed foods, purchased baked goods, margarine and shortening	• Raises blood levels of "bad" (LDL) cholesterol	• U.S. food labels list trans fats.

Nutritional values

The recipes in this book have been analyzed for significant nutrients to help you evaluate your diet and balance your meals throughout the day. Using these calculations, along with the other information in this book, you can create meals that have the optimal balance of nutrients. Having the following nutritional values at your fingertips will help you plan healthful meals.

Keep in mind that the calculations reflect nutrients per serving unless otherwise noted. Not included in the calculations are ingredients that are optional or added to taste, or those that are suggested as an alternative or substitution in the recipe, recipe note, or variation. For recipes that yield a range of servings, the calculations are for the middle of that range. Many recipes call for a specific amount of salt and also suggest seasoning food to taste; however, if you are on a low-sodium diet, it is prudent to omit salt. If you have particular concerns about any nutrient needs, consult your doctor.

The numbers for all nutritional values have been rounded using the guidelines required for reporting nutrient levels in the "Nutrition Facts" panel on U.S. food labels.

The best way to acquire the nutrients your body needs is through food. However, a balanced multivitamin-mineral supplement or a fortified cereal that does not exceed 100 percent of the daily need for any nutrient is a safe addition to your diet.

WHAT COUNTS AS A SERVING?	HOW MANY SERVINGS DO YOU NEED EACH DAY?		
	For a 1,600-calorie-per-day diet (children 2–6, sedentary women, some older adults)	For a 2,200-calorie-per-day diet (children over 6, teen girls, active women, sedentary men)	For a 2,800-calorie-per-day diet (teen boys, active men)
Fruit Group 1 medium whole fruit such as apple, orange, banana, or pear ½ cup (2–3 oz/60–90 g) chopped, cooked, or canned fruit ¼ cup (3 oz/90 g) dried fruit ¾ cup (6 fl oz/180 ml) fruit juice	2	3	4
Vegetable Group 1 cup (1 oz/30 g) raw, leafy vegetables ½ cup (2–3 oz/60–90 g) other vegetables, cooked or raw ¾ cup (6 fl oz/180 ml) vegetable juice	3	4	5
Bread, Cereal, Rice, and Pasta Group 1 slice of bread 1 cup (6 oz/180 g) ready-to-eat cereal ½ cup (2.5 oz/80 g) cooked cereal, rice, pasta	6	9	11

Adapted from USDA Dietary Guidelines (2005).

Purple & blue		CALORIES	PROTEIN/ GM	CARBS/ GM	TOT. FAT/ GM	SAT. FAT/ GM	CHOL/ MG	FIBER/ GM	SODIUM/ MG
p.23	Purple belgian endive & crab salad	198	23	2	10	1	115	1	681
p.23	Blueberry salad	232	6	12	19	5	19	3	386
p.24	Italian-style grilled eggplant	242	3	18	19	3	0	10	881
p.24	Warm purple potato salad	335	7	52	11	1	0	4	316
p.27	Roasted plums stuffed with blue cheese	206	7	22	11	5	19	2	413
p.27	Fresh fig & goat cheese salad	252	5	20	18	5	10	4	232
p.30	Purple cabbage slaw with raisins	257	7	28	14	2	0	5	712
p.30	Purple kale crostini	240	7	21	15	3	5	3	491
p.33	Purple bell pepper & goat cheese terrine	93	6	4	6	4	14	1	399
p.33	Eggplant pesto	257	7	28	14	2	0	5	712
p.34	Brie & smoked chicken with blueberry compote	211	17	8	11	4	82	1	325
p.34	Purple asparagus roasted with proscuitto	94	7	4	6	1	19	1	703

Green		CALORIES	PROTEIN/ GM	CARBS/ GM	TOT. FAT/ GM	SAT. FAT/ GM	CHOL/ MG	FIBER/ GM	SODIUM/ MG
p.41	Artichoke soup with crostini	250	15	24	13	4	13	9	555
p.41	Cucumber & feta cheese salad	157	6	6	12	4	15	2	423
p.42	Grilled zucchini skewers with coriander	141	6	13	8	1	4	3	217
p.42	Avocado, grapefruit & chive salad	321	4	23	26	4	0	9	173
p.45	Kiwifriut, apple & grape salad with rosemary syrup	141	1	37	0	0	0	3	3
p.45	Baby artichokes with black olives & lemon	335	10	47	13	2	0	8	1025
p.48	Green pears baked with stilton cheese	146	3	17	8	5	23	3	194
p.48	Open-face sandwiches with mint cream cheese	200	8	30	6	3	13	3	454
p.51	Tuna rounds with tomatillo guacamole	185	16	6	11	2	29	4	194
p.51	Celery & turkey salad	174	22	6	6	2	57	2	754
p.52	Polenta galettes with leek & swiss chard	352	9	48	15	5	17	7	1051

White & tan

		CALORIES	PROTEIN/ GM	CARBS/ GM	TOT. FAT/ GM	SAT. FAT/ GM	CHOL/ MG	FIBER/ GM	SODIUM/ MG
p.59	Mushrooms stuffed with serrano ham	137	6	5	10	2	11	1	322
p.59	Tan pear, walnut & blue cheese salad	216	5	13	17	4	11	3	490
p.60	Jerusalem artichoke soup with truffle oil	95	5	14	2	0	0	1	389
p.60	Mediterranean salad with roasted garlic dressing	299	5	20	24	3	0	7	156
p.63	Caramelized onion & shallot pissaladière	457	9	59	21	6	15	4	597
p.66	Jicama & shrimp ceviche	95	12	9	1	0	86	3	379
p.66	Sherried mushroom soup	110	8	7	5	2	8	1	228
p.69	White corn pancakes with crème fraîche	300	7	28	18	8	96	2	49
p.69	Crostini with tan figs & camembert cheese	284	11	33	13	7	31	4	486

Yellow & orange

		CALORIES	PROTEIN/ GM	CARBS/ GM	TOT. FAT/ GM	SAT. FAT/ GM	CHOL/ MG	FIBER/ GM	SODIUM/ MG
p.75	Carrot soup with fresh ginger	109	3	11	6	1	0	3	425
p.75	Cantaloupe & feta cheese salad	119	4	20	4	2	13	2	205
p.76	Persimmon & yellow apple salad	171	1	27	9	1	0	4	293
p.76	Peach & prosciutto bruschetta	82	3	10	4	1	5	1	165
p.79	Corn flans with lobster topping	193	16	14	9	4	178	1	627
p.82	Linguine with lemon & pecorino cheese	433	17	63	13	4	18	3	528
p.82	Yellow gazpacho	136	5	20	5	1	0	4	421
p.85	Orange pepper frittata with fresh thyme	246	13	4	20	6	332	1	654
p.85	Dried apricot canapés	362	13	33	21	7	39	4	408
p.86	Grapefruit, chicken & pistachio salad	244	18	15	13	2	42	3	474
p.86	Yellow beet & yellow pear tomato salad	186	7	5	16	4	12	1	223

Red		CALORIES	PROTEIN/ GM	CARBS/ GM	TOT. FAT/ GM	SAT. FAT/ GM	CHOL/ MG	FIBER/ GM	SODIUM/ MG
p.93	Smoked trout salad with blood orange dressing	133	11	11	5	1	28	1	12
p.93	Red apple, walnut & stilton salad	253	5	26	16	4	14	6	407
p.94	Red onion marmalade & pork canapés	378	16	32	18	5	50	2	170
p.97	Grapes with roquefort & almond coating	231	11	9	18	6	26	2	522
p.97	Red beet pancakes with yogurt & dill	127	6	16	5	1	72	2	284
p.100	Roasted tomato soup with basil	302	5	24	23	3	0	6	777
p.100	Watermelon, raspberry & mint salad	114	2	28	1	0	0	7	5
p.103	Ruby grapefruit & pomegranate salad	157	2	23	7	1	0	2	149
p.103	Smoked gouda toasts with rhubarb chutney	504	10	96	11	4	37	3	412
p.104	Roasted red potato canapés with salmon roe	114	3	10	7	2	38	1	234
p.104	Prosciutto-wrapped radicchio wedges	109	6	2	9	2	15	0	314

Brown		CALORIES	PROTEIN/ GM	CARBS/ GM	TOT. FAT/ GM	SAT. FAT/ GM	CHOL/ MG	FIBER/ GM	SODIUM/ MG
p.111	Pork satay with peanut sauce (2 Tbsp sauce)	347	27	9	23	9	68	2	634
p.112	Black bean & fresh corn tostadas	221	10	33	6	1	1	9	329
p.112	Split pea soup with tarragon cream	304	19	47	5	1	5	19	607
p.115	Quinoa & grilled summer vegetables	414	9	43	24	3	0	7	1352
p.118	Bulgur salad with lemon, peas & mint	212	7	34	7	1	0	9	665
p.118	Millet salad with mango & cilantro	514	14	98	7	1	0	6	300
p.121	White bean & sage crostini	352	6	32	21	3	0	5	1001
p.121	Orzo salad with cucumber	322	10	43	13	2	0	4	307
p.122	Hummus with pita points	440	10	52	21	3	0	6	854
p.122	Lentil soup	268	18	46	2	0	3	12	714
p.125	Buckwheat pancakes with tomato-corn salsa	265	8	29	14	2	57	5	560

Glossary

apples: The major portion of the apple's nutrition is in its skin, which contains the flavonoid quercetin, an antioxidant that fights viruses and allergies and is thought to be an anticarcinogenic. Apple flesh is an important source of pectin, a fiber that lowers cholesterol.

apricots: The apricot's color is due to the pigments beta-carotene and lycopene, which promote eye health and heart health, lower the risk of some cancers, and strengthen the immune system. Apricots are also high in vitamin C, potassium, and fiber.

artichokes: The artichoke's fleshy heart provides a complex of heart-healthy phytochemicals, including cynarin; it also contains chlorophyll and beta-carotene and provides a wide range of vitamins and minerals.

arugula (rocket): A bitter green, arugula is eaten both cooked and raw. It is a good source of iron and vitamins A and C and contains lutein, which protects eye health.

asparagus: This vegetable is one of the best sources of folate, a B vitamin that helps fight heart disease. It is also rich in phytochemicals, especially the flavonoid rutin, and a host of vitamins and minerals.

avocados: Technically a fruit, the avocado is high in fat, but most of it is monounsaturated, which helps to lower cholesterol. It also contains beta-sitosterol, a plant cholesterol that lowers cholesterol as well, and may prevent the growth of cancer cells. Avocados are high in vitamins and minerals, especially vitamins A, C, folate, B_6, and potassium.

bananas: Bananas are especially high in potassium, which balances sodium and helps regulate blood pressure, and may reduce arterial plaque formation. Potassium also helps to prevent strokes by lowering platelet activity and reducing blood clots. Bananas are also high in vitamins C and B_6, and contain a kind of fiber that may protect against colon cancer.

barley: Hulled barley, Scotch barley (coarsely ground), and grits (cracked) retain their bran and germ, and so provide the antioxidant selenium. Pearl barley, which has been refined, steamed, and polished, lacks the nutrients of these whole grains.

basil: Traditionally used in kitchens throughout the Mediterranean and in Southeast Asia, basil is one of the world's best-loved herbs and is a source of green phytonutrients. Although related to mint, basil tastes faintly of anise and cloves. Italian cooks use it in pesto, often pair it with tomatoes, and consider it essential to a classic minestrone. In Thailand and Vietnam, basil is often combined with fresh mint for seasoning stir-fries, curries, and salads.

bay leaf: Elongated gray-green leaves used to flavor sauces, soups, stews, and braises, imparting a slightly sweet, citrusy, nutty flavor. Usually sold dried, bay leaves should be removed from a dish before serving, as they are leathery and can have sharp edges.

beans, black: Also called turtle beans, these have a robust taste and are popular in Mexican cuisine. Like all dried beans, black beans contain protein, iron, calcium, and phosphorus; they are especially high in fiber.

beans, cannellini: These ivory-colored kidney beans, used in Italian cooking, have a buttery texture and a delicate taste. Great Northern beans may be substituted.

beans, kidney: Shaped like the organ that gives them their name, red kidney beans are meaty and have a more assertive flavor than white kidney beans (cannellini beans).

beets: Red beets get their color from the phytochemical betacyanin, which is believed to reduce tumor growth. They also contain betaine, which helps protect the heart, and salicic acid, which has anti-inflammatory properties, and are especially high in folate. The phytochemicals in golden beets help promote eye health and boost immunity.

Belgian endive (chicory/witloof): A member of the chicory family, Belgian endive is blanched (grown in darkness) to prevent it from turning green. It does contain phytochemicals based on the color of the tips, purple or green.

bell peppers (capsicums): All bell peppers are high in cancer-fighting phytochemicals; the various compounds that give them their different colors also promote eye health (green, yellow, orange, and red); the antioxidants in purple bell peppers aid memory function and promote healthy aging. Red peppers are high in vitamin C.

blueberries: These native American berries are so high in antioxidant and anti-inflammatory compounds that they are considered "brain food": they contain a range of anthocyanins, which are thought to help fight cancer and have antiaging capabilities. Blueberries are available fresh, dried, and frozen.

bok choy: Eaten for both its white bulb and its green leaves, bok choy is a type of cabbage and contains the same cancer-fighting compounds and a range of vitamins and minerals.

broccoli: Extremely high in vitamin C (½ cup/ 2 oz/60 g provides 68 percent of the Daily Value) and even higher in vitamin K, broccoli also contains vitamin A and cancer-fighting phytochemicals. Broccoli sprouts also contain high levels of these compounds.

broccoli rabe: With its long, thin stalks and small flowering heads, broccoli rabe has an assertive, bitter flavor. It contains many of the same nutrients as broccoli.

Brussels sprouts: These miniature green cabbages contain the same cancer-fighting compounds as their larger cousins, and are even higher in vitamin C and K than broccoli; just 4 Brussels sprouts contain 243 percent of the daily value of vitamin K, which promotes proper blood clotting.

bulgur wheat: Like other whole grains, bulgur wheat is rich in selenium, an antioxidant that is believed to fight cancer. Bulgur wheat kernels have been steamed, dried, and crushed, and are available in various grinds.

cabbage: The patriarch of the cruciferous vegetable family, cabbage is high in vitamins C and K, but its real value is its concentration of isothiocyanates, powerful cancer-fighting compounds. Red cabbage, which is actually purple, contains more vitamin C than green cabbage, along with the antioxidant anthocyanin.

capers: A Mediterranean shrub is the source of these small unopened flower buds. The buds are bitter when raw; once they are dried and packed in brine or salt, they are used to add a pleasantly pungent flavor to a variety of dishes. Capers should be rinsed before use to remove excess brine or salt.

carrots: One carrot provides a whopping 330 percent of the Daily Value of vitamin A, which is the source of its fame as a protector of eye health. Carrots are also high in fiber and the bioflavonoids and carotenoids that lower the risk of some cancers, protect the heart, and boost immunity. Maroon and purple carrots are colorful alternatives to the common orange carrot, offering different phytochemical benefits, and these colors of carrot are becoming more widely available.

cauliflower: Another member of the cruciferous family, cauliflower was traditionally blanched, or covered during growing, to keep the head white; now it has been bred to be naturally white. Even so, it still contains the cancer-fighting compounds of its cousins, along with phytochemicals that promote hearth health. Purple cauliflower offers a colorful change of pace from the common white cauliflower.

celery: Like other green vegetables, celery helps to fight certain cancers, promotes eye health, strengthens the immune system, and helps build strong bones and teeth. It is also high in fiber.

cheese, blue: These cheeses are inoculated with the spores of special molds to develop a fine network of blue veins for a strong, sharp, peppery flavor and a crumbly texture. Most blue cheeses can be crumbled, diced, spread, and sliced. Depending on the cheese's moisture content, however, some hold their shape when sliced better than others.

cheese, feta: Young cheese traditionally made from sheep's milk and used in Greek cuisine. It is known for its crumbly texture; some versions are also creamy. Feta's saltiness is heightened by the brine in which the cheese is pickled. Feta is also produced from cow's or goat's milk. Reduced-fat feta is also available.

cherries: Tart red and sweet dark red cherries derive their color from anthocyanin pigments and other antioxidants, which help protect the heart and brain, lower the risk of some cancers, and are powerful anti-inflammatories. Both sweet and tart cherries also contain a terpenoid that appears to prevent the growth of tumors.

chickpeas (garbanzo beans): These crumpled-looking dried beans are meaty and hearty-flavored when cooked. They are popular in soups and purées, and are the basis for hummus, the Middle Eastern dip.

chiles: All chiles contain the phytochemical capsaicin, which gives them their hot taste and also acts as a cancer fighter. Although usually eaten only in small amounts, they are nutrient rich, containing vitamins A, C, and E, along with folic acid and potassium.

chives: These slender, bright green stems are used to give an onionlike flavor without the bite. The slender, hollow, grasslike leaves can be snipped with a pair of kitchen scissors to any length and scattered over scrambled eggs, stews, salads, soups, tomatoes, or any dish that would benefit from a boost of mild oniony flavor. Chives do not take well to long cooking—they lose flavor and crispness and turn a dull, grayish green.

cilantro: Also called fresh coriander and Chinese parsley, cilantro is a distinctly flavored herb with legions of loyal followers. Used extensively in the cuisines of Mexico, the Caribbean, India, Egypt, Thailand, Vietnam, and China, cilantro asserts itself with a flavor that can't be missed. Some describe its taste as being citrusy or minty; others find hints of sage and parsley; some detractors describe it as soapy. It is best used fresh, added at the end of cooking, as it loses flavor after long exposure to heat.

corn: Corn is rich in vitamins, minerals, protein, and fiber. Yellow corn is given its color by carotenoids that not only fight heart disease and cancer, but also protect against macular degeneration.

couscous: A pasta made from high-protein durum wheat, couscous is also available in whole-wheat (wholemeal) form, which cooks just as quickly and is virtually indistinguishable from regular couscous.

cranberries: High in both fiber and vitamin C, cranberries are excellent for preventing urinary tract infections due to their polyphenols. The anthocyanins that make cranberries red have antioxidant properties that protect the heart and may guard against cancer. Fresh, frozen, and dried cranberries, as well as cranberry juice, are all equally beneficial to health.

crème fraîche: A soured, cultured cream product originating in France, crème fraîche is similar to sour cream. The silken, thick cream, which is 30 percent fat, is tangy and sweet, with a hint of nuttiness. It adds incomparable flavor when used as a topping for berries and pastry desserts. It is also delicious paired with smoked salmon and trout, and lends a velvety smoothness and rich flavor to soups and sauces. Crème fraîche is not always easy to find and many home cooks make their own from heavy cream and buttermilk.

cucumbers: A member of the gourd family, the most commonly available cucumber is sold with a waxed coating, which must be peeled, thus removing the beneficial phytochemicals of its skin. The unwaxed, thinner skin of English (hothouse) cucumbers can be eaten, as can that of Armenian cucumbers, similar to English cucumbers but smaller.

currants, dried black: Dried black currants are actually dried Zante grapes. Although smaller than raisins, they have most of the same nutrients.

dates: Occasionally available fresh in late summer and early fall, dates are more commonly found dried, when their high sugar content increases greatly. They also provide iron and protein.

dill: The fine, feathery leaves of this herb have a distinct aromatic flavor. Dill is used in savory pastries, baked vegetables, and, of course, in the making of pickles.

eggplants (aubergines): The purple skin of the familiar globe eggplant is rich in heart- and brain-healthy anthocyanins, while its flesh contains saponins, antioxidants that help to lower cholesterol levels. Other varieties may be slightly smaller and have lavender, white,

rose, green, or variegated skin. The color of the eggplant's skin does not determine the flavor.

fennel seeds: The seed of the common fennel has a licorice-like flavor and may be used ground or whole in savory dishes such as bouillabaisse, sausage, and pork stews and roasts. It is also used in some breads and desserts and to flavor liqueurs.

figs: Whether fresh (available in summer and early fall) or dried, figs provide phosphorus, calcium, and iron.

garlic: Unusually rich in antioxidants and anti-inflammatories, garlic forms organosulfur compounds when chopped, crushed, or sliced. These substances lower blood pressure, slow clotting, and promote heart health.

ginger: Prized in Chinese cuisine for its culinary and medicinal uses, ginger aids digestion and lowers cholesterol. It contains both antioxidant and antimicrobial compounds.

grapefruit: Half a grapefruit provides 70 percent of Daily Value of vitamin C. Pink or red grapefruits are high in vitamin A as well. Both yellow and pink types contain flavonoids that help guard against cancer, while the latter also has lycopene, which boosts that activity.

grapes: The dark purple Concord grape, which is usually made into grape juice, is extremely high in antioxidants, making grape juice an important heart-healthy food. Red table grapes also promote heart health and immunity, and green grapes can help lower cancer risk and promote eye health.

green beans: Providing both vitamins A and C, green beans also protect eye health because of their lutein content.

green (spring) onions: Like all onions, green onions contain organosulfur compounds, which are thought to protect the heart and improve the good/bad cholesterol ratio.

ham, serrano: Ham is a portion of the lean hind leg of a pig that has been cured, or preserved, and flavored, often by smoking. The curing is done by various methods, depending on the style of ham. Traditional European hams, like Italian prosciutto and Spanish serrano, are dry-cured in salt and air-dried.

Jerusalem artichokes (sunchokes): Although they are not true artichokes but a kind of sunflower, these tubers have a nutty taste slightly reminiscent of artichokes. They are particularly high in iron and may be eaten either raw or cooked.

jicama: Technically a legume, crisp and nutty jicama is eaten both raw and cooked. It provides vitamin C and potassium.

juniper berries: These attractive blue-black berries, the size of small peas, are harvested from the evergreen juniper bush. They are added to marinades used to flavor assertive-tasting meats such as rabbit, lamb, and venison. Their best-known use is to flavor gin.

kale: Another member of the wide-ranging cruciferous vegetable family, kale shares their cancer-fighting abilities. A half cup serving is high in vitamin A (96 percent of Daily Value), and contains a spectacular amount of vitamin K (590 percent of Daily Value!). It has more beta-carotene than broccoli and is an important source of lutein, which promotes eye health.

kiwifruits: Extremely high in vitamin C (two kiwifruits contain 240 percent of Daily Value, almost twice as much as an orange), these fruits are also high in folate and potassium.

kumquats: These tiny oval orange citrus fruits are like backward oranges: their peel is sweet and their flesh is sour. Often candied or used sliced as an accent or as a garnish, they are high in vitamin A, vitamin C, and potassium.

leeks: By virtue of their membership in the onion family, leeks contain organosulfur compounds, which are thought to fight cancer and heart disease. They also help improve the body's good-bad cholesterol ratio.

lemons: High in vitamin C, lemons are a flavor enhancer; add lemon juice to raw and cooked fruits and use it to replace salt at the table for vegetables and fish.

lentils: High in protein, like all beans, lentils come in a wide variety of colors. They also provide iron, phosphorus, calcium, and vitamins A and B.

lettuces: The many types of lettuce can be divided into four major groups: butterhead, crisphead, leaf, and romaine (cos). Most lettuces are high in vitamins A and C; they also provide calcium and iron. The darker the green of the lettuce, the higher the level of its beneficial phytochemicals, which include the eye-protectant lutein.

limes: High in vitamin C, like all citrus fruits, lime juice also contains lutein, which benefits eye health. The Persian lime is widely available, while the yellowish-green Key lime is usually found fresh only in Florida and some specialty produce markets. The juice is available in bottles.

melons: Higher in healthful nutrients than any other melon, the cantaloupe is also rich in vitamins A and C and potassium. It is heart healthy and helps to lower the risk of cancer, thanks to its beta-carotene content. A wide variety of other orange-fleshed melons are also available. Green-fleshed honeydew melons and Persian melons contain cancer-fighting phytochemicals as well.

millet: These pale yellow, spherical, mild-flavored grains are cooked in liquid and swell considerably in size to make a side dish or breakfast cereal popular in southern Europe, northern Africa, and Asia.

mint: A refreshing herb available in many varieties, with spearmint the most common. Used fresh to flavor a broad range of savory preparations, including spring lamb, poultry, and vegetables, or to garnish desserts.

mushrooms: Not vegetables or fruits but fungi, mushrooms come in a variety of forms and are available both wild and cultivated. They are rich in riboflavin, niacin, and pantothenic acid, all B-complex vitamins, and also contain the valuable minerals copper and selenium.

nectarines: A relative of the peach, the nectarine has the advantage of an edible skin that contains many of its phytochemicals. Yellow nectarines contain beta-carotene, while the pink-skinned, white-fleshed variety has its own group of beneficial compounds.

nuts: High in fiber, nuts also contain folate, riboflavin, and magnesium. They are high in beneficial omega-3 fatty acids and vitamin E, an antioxidant that protects brain cells, promotes heart health, and lowers LDL (bad) cholesterol.

oats: Oat groats are whole grains that may be cut into pieces to make Scotch, steel-cut, or Irish oats, or steamed and rolled into old-fashioned, or rolled, oats. When the groats are cut into pieces and rolled thinner, they become quick-cooking oats. All of these forms retain their selenium and cholesterol-fighting nutrients, unlike instant oats. They are also high in vitamins B_1, B_6, and E.

onions: All onions contain organosulfur compounds that are thought to fight cancer and to promote heart health. Yellow and red onions also contain quercetin, which boosts these actions, while red onions have the added benefit of the antioxidant anthocyanin.

oranges: Famed for their high vitamin C content, oranges are also high in folate and potassium. They also provide limonoids and flavonoids, two disease-fighting antioxidants.

peaches: While its fuzzy skin is usually not eaten, the yellow or white flesh of the peach contains the vitamins A and C. Peaches are available either freestone or clingstone and can be found fresh, dried, frozen, and canned.

peanuts: Although they are not truly nuts, but legumes, peanuts are high in fat. They are a good source of protein, but they should be eaten in small amounts. Like most nuts, the fat they contain is largely monounsaturated.

pears: The beneficial pigments of pears are concentrated in their skin; as the skin is quite thin (except in the tan-skinned varieties), they can be eaten unpeeled, whether raw or cooked. The flesh contains vitamin A, as well as some phosphorus.

peas, English: Also called green, or garden, peas, they should be eaten soon after picking; they are also available frozen. They provide niacin and iron, along with vitamins A and C.

peas, split: When dried, the yellow or green field pea may be split at its natural seam for faster cooking in soups or purées. They are especially high in fiber and contain vitamin A.

peas, sugar snap: A cross between the English pea and the snow pea (mangetout), sugar snaps resemble the former but are entirely edible either cooked or raw. They provide vitmains A and C, along with folate, iron, phosphorus, and thiamin.

persimmons: Both the small, squat Fuyu, which is eaten when hard and crisp, and the larger, slightly pointed Hachiya, which is eaten when fully ripe, are rich in beta-carotenes and vitamin C.

pineapples: The pineapple's sweet, juicy flesh provides manganese, vitamins A and C, and bromelain, an antiflammatory enzyme that is also a digestive aid.

pine nuts: Delicate, buttery pine nuts contain both iron and thiamin. They are a favored garnish for salads and cooked foods.

plums: The edible skin of the plum, which comes in a variety of colors, contains most of its phytochemicals, although the yellow, purple, or red flesh also contains beneficial compounds. A good source of vitamin C, plums are one of the most healthful fruits. When they are not in season, enjoy them as prunes, their dried form.

polenta (corn): Although polenta may be made from other dried grains or white corn, usually it is coarsely or finely ground yellow cornmeal. Only stone-ground cornmeal is whole grain; store it in an airtight container in the refrigerator.

pomegranates: The fleshy seeds of this fruit are high in vitamin C, potassium, and heart-healthy anthocyanins. The fruit is in season during the fall months, while pomegranate juice is available year-round in natural foods stores and some other markets.

potatoes: The deeper the color of its pigment, the more healthful phytochemicals a potato possesses, but all potatoes are extremely rich in vitamins and minerals if eaten with the skin; they are also high in fiber. Make sure to buy organic potatoes; commercially grown potatoes contain high levels of pesticides.

prunes: These dried prune plums, now also called dried plums, are rich in vitamin A, potassium, and fiber. They are higher in antioxidants than any other fruit or vegetable, making them the top antiaging food.

pumpkins: The flesh of the pumpkin is nutrient rich with vitamin A and carotenoids, specifically the cancer-fighters alpha- and beta-carotene and lutein.

pumpkin seeds: High in fiber, protein, and various minerals, pumpkin seeds also contain beta-sisterol, which lowers cholesterol and slows the growth of abnormal cells. Clean and toast your own, or buy them in natural foods stores or Latino markets.

quinoa: An ancient Incan grain, quinoa is higher in protein than all other grains, and its protein is complete. It is also rich in nutrients and unsaturated fat.

radicchio: A red-leafed member of the chicory family, radicchio comes in the loose-headed Verona variety and the tighter, more rounded Treviso variety. Both kinds have an assertive, bitter flavor, and both provide beneficial antioxidants such as anthocyanins and lycopene. Radicchio may be eaten raw, grilled, baked, or sautéed.

radishes: These peppery roots belong in the mustard family and are available in a variety of colors. They contain vitamin C and cancer-fighting antioxidants.

raisins: Antioxidant rich, raisins are also high in vitamins, minerals, and fiber. Both dark raisins and golden raisins (sultanas) start as green grapes, but golden raisins are treated with sulfur dioxide to prevent oxidation.

raspberries: Red raspberries have more fiber than most other fruits; they are also high in vitamin C and folate and extremely high in cancer-fighting antioxidants. Golden raspberries are less common, but they contain heart- and eye-healthy bioflavonoids. Although fresh raspberries are fragile, frozen unsweetened raspberries retain their flavor and are available year-round.

rhubarb: These tart red stalks are one of the first signs of spring when they appear in the market. High in vitamin A and beneficial phytochemicals, rhubarb helps protect the heart, boost immunity, and lower the risk of some cancers.

rice, brown: This whole grain retains its bran covering, making it high in fiber. Brown rice is available in long-, medium-, and short- grain varieties. Like other whole grains, it is high in fiber and selenium; because the bran can become rancid at room temperature, brown rice it should be kept refrigerated.

rosemary: Used fresh or dried, this Mediterranean herb has a strong, fragrant flavor well suited to meats, poultry, seafood, and vegetables. It is a particularly good complement to roasted chicken and lamb.

rutabagas: Another member of the cabbage family, this yellow-skinned root vegetable has a mild-tasting yellow flesh. It contains vitamins A and C, as well as fiber and potassium.

sesame seeds: Flat and minute, sesame seeds come in several colors, but are most commonly a light ivory. They are rich in manganese, copper, and calcium, and also contain cholesterol-lowering lignans. Because they have a high oil content, they should be kept refrigerated. Toasting them briefly in a dry frying pan brings out their flavor.

shallots: Another onion family member, the shallot contains the same heart-healthy organosulfides as its relatives. It is milder in taste and more convenient to use in small amounts than the onion.

snow peas (mangetouts): Once both tips are pinched off, the thin, delicate snow pea is completely edible, either raw or cooked. It provides both calcium and iron.

spinach: High in a multitude of nutrients, from vitamins A, C, and K to folate and potassium, spinach is also one of the best sources of lutein, the carotenoid that prevents macular degeneration.

squash, summer: Most of the summer squash's nutrients are contained in its bright, edible yellow skin. It is a good source of manganese, as well as the carotenoids that give it its color.

squash, winter: The dense, meaty flesh of winter squashes is rich with vitamins A and C, folate, manganese, and potassium, as well as heart-protective and cancer-fighting carotenoids.

strawberries: Rich in antioxidant content, partly due to their anthocyanin pigments, strawberries are also extremely high in vitamin C. Because of these compounds, as well as their phenolic acids, these berries are thought to be important cancer-fighters.

sweet potatoes: The most commonly available of these root vegetables are a pale yellow variety and a dark orange one often erroneously referred to as a yam. Both are high in fiber, vitamins A and C, and a host of other vitamins and minerals, as well as more beta-carotene than any other vegetable.

Swiss chard: Yet another member of the far-flung cruciferous vegetable family, chard has dark green leaves and either white or red stalks and ribs. Along with cancer-fighting phytochemicals, it contains iron and vitamins A and C.

tomatillos: Sometimes called Mexican green tomatoes, tomatillos are firmer and less juicy than tomatoes and grow to ripeness inside a pale-green papery sheath. Used both raw and cooked, they are an essential sweet-sour ingredient in many Mexican green sauces. Look for fresh or canned tomatillos in well-stocked supermarkets or Latin groceries.

tomatoes: Not only are tomatoes high in vitamin C, they are also high in fiber and have good amounts of other vitamins and minerals. Tomatoes also contain lycopene, which lowers cancer risk. The body absorbs this antioxidant better when tomatoes are cooked, making tomato sauce and tomato paste especially healthful.

vinegar: Many types are available, made from a variety of red or white wines or, like cider vinegar and rice vinegar, from fruits and grains. Vinegars are further seasoned by infusing them with fresh herbs, fruit, garlic, or other flavorful ingredients. All offer a healthful, low-fat way to season a range of foods.

watercress: This spicy green is, surprisingly, a cruciferous vegetable. It contains good amounts of vitamins A and C. The peppery taste of watercress is due to a certain isothiocyanate that has shown the potential to help combat lung cancer.

watermelon: Despite its high water content, this melon provides vitamins A and C, along with the anthocyanins that give it its color.

wheat, whole (wholemeal): The bran in whole wheat contains selenium and other minerals, as well as vitamin E. Whole wheat is also an important source of fiber, which is thought to help lower the risk of strokes and heart disease. As with all whole grains, all forms of whole wheat, from wheat germ to flour, should be kept refrigerated.

wine: The colors of red and rosé wines are due to the skins of the purple grapes used to make the wines; red wine has more beneficial flavonoids than grape juice. These phytochemicals have been shown to help increase "good" HDL cholesterol.

yogurt: The bacterial cultures in yogurt are prized as an aid in digestion. Like the milk it is made from, yogurt can be full fat, low fat, or nonfat.

zucchini (courgettes): Most of the zucchini's nutrients are found in its skin, which contains phytochemicals that strengthen the eyes, bones, and teeth; help to boost immunity; and lower the risk of some cancers.

Bibliography

The resources below were used in the creation of this book, and are recommended for further reading on the subject of colorful plant foods:

BOOKS

Gollman, Barbara, and Kim Pierce. *The Phytopia Cookbook*. Dallas, Tex.: Phytopia, Inc., 1998.

Green, Eliza. *Field Guide to Produce*. Philadephia: Quirk Books, 2004.

Heber, David, M.D., Ph.D. *What Color Is Your Diet?* New York: Harper Collins, 2001.

Hess, Mary Abbott, L.H.D., M.S., R.D., F.A.D.A.; Dana Jacobi; and Marie Simmons. *Williams-Sonoma Essentials of Healthful Cooking*. Menlo Park, Calif.: Oxmoor House, 2003.

Joseph, James A., Ph.D.; Daniel A. Nadeau, M.D.; and Anne Underwood. *The Color Code*. New York: Hyperion, 2002.

Pivonka, Elizabeth, R.D., Ph.D., and Barbara Berry, M.S., R.D. *5 a Day: The Better Health Cookbook*. New York: Rodale, 2002.

Tantillo, Tony, and Sam Gugino. *Eat Fresh, Stay Healthy*. New York: Macmillan General Reference, 1997.

WEBSITES

Centers for Disease Control: http://www.cdc.gov

National Cancer Institute: http://www.nci.nih.gov

Produce for Better Health Foundation: http://www.5aday.org

United States Department of Agriculture: http://www.usda.gov

University of California, Berkeley, School of Public Health Wellness Letter: http://www.wellnessletter.com

Index

FREE PRESS

A Division of Simon & Schuster, Inc.
1230 Avenue of the Americas
New York, NY 10020

WILLIAMS-SONOMA

Founder & Vice-Chairman Chuck Williams

WELDON OWEN INC.

Chief Executive Officer John Owen

President and Chief Operating Officer Terry Newell

Chief Financial Officer Christine E. Munson

Vice President International Sales Stuart Laurence

Creative Director Gaye Allen

Publisher Hannah Rahill

Associate Publisher Sarah Putman Clegg

Editor Emily Miller

Editorial Assistant Juli Vendzules

Photo Director and Senior Designer Marisa Kwek

Production Director Chris Hemesath

Color Manager Teri Bell

Production and Reprint Coordinator Todd Rechner

THE WILLIAMS-SONOMA NEW HEALTHY KITCHEN *STARTERS*

Conceived and produced by Weldon Owen Inc.
814 Montgomery Street, San Francisco, CA 94133
Telephone: 415 291 0100 Fax: 415 291 8841

In collaboration with Williams-Sonoma, Inc.
3250 Van Ness Avenue, San Francisco, CA 94109

A WELDON OWEN PRODUCTION
Copyright © 2006 by Weldon Owen Inc. and Williams-Sonoma Inc.

For information regarding special discounts for bulk purchases, please contact Simon & Schuster Special Sales at 1-800-456-6798 or business@simonandschuster.com

Set in Vectora

Color separations by Mission Productions Limited.
Printed and bound in Hong Kong by Midas Printing.

First printed in 2005.

10 9 8 7 6 5 4 3 2

Library of Congress Cataloging-in-Publication data is available.

ISBN-13: 978-0-7432-7858-4
ISBN-10: 0-7432-7858-5

ACKNOWLEDGMENTS

Weldon Owen wishes to thank the following people for their generous support in producing this book:
Copy Editor Carolyn Miller; **Consulting Editor** Judith Dunham; **Proofreaders** Desne Ahlers and Carrie Bradley; **Indexer** Ken DellaPenta; Adrienne Aquino; Shadin Saah; Carol Hacker; Jackie Mills; Marianne Mitten; and Richard Yu.

Photographer Dan Goldberg

Photographer's Assistant Julie Caine

Food Stylist Jen Straus

Assistant Food Stylist Max La Rivière-Hedrick

Photographer Ben Dearnley

Food and Prop Stylist Julz Beresford

Assistant Food Stylist Jess Sly

The images on the following pages were created by this photo team:
8–9; 18 *top left, top right, bottom right;* 22; 25; 28; 29 *bottom;* 31; 32; 36; 39; 43; 44; 46; 47; 49; 50; 53; 54; 57; 58; 61; 62; 64; 65; 67; 68; 70 *top left, top right;* 74; 77; 80; 81 *top;* 87; 88; 91; 92; 95; 96; 98; 99 *top;* 102; 105; 106 *bottom left, bottom right;* 113; 114; 117 *top;* 119; 120; 123.

The images on the following pages were created by this photo team:
18 *bottom left;* 21; 26; 29 *top;* 35; 40; 70 *bottom left, bottom right;* 73; 78; 81 *bottom;* 83; 84; 99 *bottom;* 101; 106 *top left, top right;* 109; 110; 116; 117 *bottom;* 124.

A NOTE ON WEIGHTS AND MEASURES

All recipes include customary U.S. and metric measurements. Metric conversions are based on a standard developed for these books and have been rounded off. Actual weights may vary.